GET YOUR KICKS ON THE A456

First published May 2005

Published by: John Combe Associates, 8 Wolverley Road, Kidderminster, DY1 5JN

Printed by: Stargold Limited, Digital House, Stourport Road, Kidderminster.

*   Every effort has been made to contact the copyright holders of the Tornados photographs

INTRODUCTION
by John Combe

At midnight on New Years Eve 1999 I stood outside my local pub pint in hand, looking at the rockets flying skywards to celebrate the new millennium and thinking about all the great groups that had originated from Kidderminster over the last forty years or so. I mentioned this to a few friends and it was generally decided in a moment of drunken bonhomie that I ought to write a book about it. Although it crossed my mind over the next few weeks the idea had quietly been shelved, when I was asked "Have you started the book yet". Toying with the idea I finally made my mind up to bite the bullet and give it a go. Over the next couple of years I worked on the book and all was generally going well when in October 2002, disaster struck. I was rushed to hospital in Worcester with persistent hiccups and flu and put into intensive care before being transferred to the City Hospital in Birmingham, due to a lack of beds in Worcester! I came round about a month later to find that I had a viral infection which had given me pneumonia and paralysis in my legs. After ten months of rehabilitation I was transferred to Cookley Ward in Kidderminster, finally leaving hopsital in August 2003. This time I left in a wheelchair. For a few weeks the book was the last thing on my mind, but with encouragement I eventually managed to pick up the pieces and worked on the book throughout 2004.

The book is in three chapters covering distinct periods. The chapters are divided into three parts. Part one is a story of the period which can be followed right through, and part two contains mini-biographies of the groups active at the time. Part three lists events that happened during that era and are mostly connected to the music scene although as I trawled through old copies of the Kidderminster Shuttle could not help but be reminded of the drastic changes the town has gone through. Kidderminster has never been a particularly picturesque placc but it retained a certain kind of Victorian, Dickensian charm. This was nearly all swept away during the 1960s with the building of the ring road and development of the Swan Centre, so I have made a note of some of these changes and included some events that interested or amused me.

I could not have completed this book without the help of Tricia Roberts who has been of tremendous assistance and would also Like to thank Dave Cartwright for proof reading and Terry Salters and the design team at

Stargold printers. Finally I would like to thank Hazel and Charlotte my wife and daughter who have supported and encouraged me through the difficult times.

Enjoy the book and support live music, both the big acts and groups playing locall. (There are still a few venues left, The Talbot, Bewdley; The Tap House, Worcester Street, Kidderminster and the Queens Head at Wolverly.)

Liberate your body. Liberate your soul. ROCK 'N' ROLL!

John Combe, May 2005

To Mick,

Best Wishes
John.

Front cover illustration by Charlotte Combe,
pictured with author John Combe.

CONTENTS

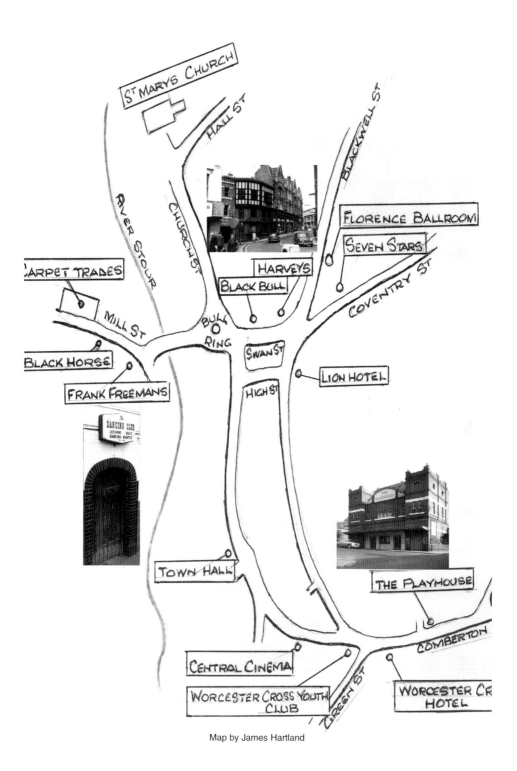

St Marys Church

Hall St

Blackwell St

River Stour

Church St

Florence Ballroom

Seven Stars

Carpet Trades

Harveys

Black Bull

Coventry St

Mill St

Bull Ring

Black Horse

Swan St

Lion Hotel

Frank Freemans

High St

Town Hall

The Playhouse

Comberton

Central Cinema

Green St

Worcester Cross Youth Club

Worcester Cr Hotel

Map by James Hartland

vi

CHAPTER ONE
THE ROCK 'N' ROLL YEARS

1956 - 1962

If you ever plan to motor west out of Birmingham city centre, take the A456 driving past the Clent Hills, Hagley and Blakedown. Some seventeen miles later you will arrive in Kidderminster which together with its smaller neighbours of Stourport and Bewdley makes up the district of Wyre Forest, named after the ancient deciduous forest which spreads

westwards from the outskirts of Bewdley towards Cleobury Mortimer and the Welsh Marches.

With a little stretch of the imagination, Kidderminster could be compared to the ancient city of Rome inasmuch as it is surrounded by hills with a river running through it.

Admittedly Kidderminster only has four hills compared to Rome's seven: Comberton Hill, Bewdley Hill, Sion Hill and Rowland Hill, while the River Stour is Kidderminster's

THE SKIFFLE KINGS at the Thurston Hotel, Bewdley

answer to the Tiber. Here however any similarity ends. Kidderminster has never had an empire extending across the entire known world but its excellent carpets have covered millions of square miles of the earth's surface and its singers and musicians have entertained millions of people across the globe. It is to these musicians that this book is dedicated, both the famous and the obscure.

Our story begins in Bewdley, a town too posh to be an inland port, it left that honour to Stourport. It was on a Friday night in the spring of 1956 that the immortal words *"It Takes A Worried Man To Sing A Worried Song"* could be heard from the inside of the Thurston Hotel, a crusty old Georgian watering hole situated on the banks of the River Severn. They were being sung by Tony Goodwin, singer with the newly formed 'Severn Valley Skiffle Kings'.

They had been hired by the landlord Jack Griffin, who had advertised for a pianist and got offered a six piece skiffle band instead. Their success was instant, and when Tony got married on June 6th in Wribbenhall Parish Church, hordes of their fans turned up to wish them well.

Their popularity was not surprising, the times were ripe for a change! In the ballrooms and dance schools of the area, strict tempo dance bands were the order of the day, and would stay on the live music scene for a few years to come. 'The Jimmy Aldridge Band' at The Florence and 'The Carlton Orchestra' at The Black Horse were typical of the era.

So for the first year of their existence, 'The Skiffle Kings' held sway as the only band for teenagers in the area. For a while a trio of servicemen from the military camp at Wolverley called 'The Skivers' appeared on the scene and were rated pretty hot. 'The Skiffle Kings' and 'The Skivers' in fact appeared together on the same bill, when the ever enterprising Frank Freeman had organised a rock 'n' roll skiffle ball at the Town Hall in September 1957. However, 'The Skivers' soon left the area, and 'The Skiffle Kings' once again reigned supreme. But competition was arriving. Other youngsters were taking notice, Terry Salters had seen 'The Skiffle Kings' at The Tontine in Stourport. Inspired by them, together with a few friends, he formed 'The Danville Saints'. They rehearsed at The Worcester Cross Youth Club, run by a Mr Henderson, which had an amplifier and microphone that the lads could use. Worcester Cross Youth Club helped many youngsters start up bands in this era.

Another young lad who had noticed Tony Goodwin was twelve year old Nick Miller, son of a local policeman in Bewdley, who spotted Tony one day walking past his house, guitar hanging around his neck. Nick was impressed, they got talking and even singing a few songs. The outcome was that Nick pressurised his dad into buying him a guitar.

Nick learnt fast, four months later he did his first professional booking as a solo artist at the Lax Lane school dance on a Saturday night in January 1957. The following Saturday he appeared at Wribbenhall Parish Rooms with his hero Tony Goodwin.

This led Nick to joining 'The Saddletramps,' an aspiring skiffle, rock 'n' roll group, with lots of enthusiasm and very little equipment, who had taken over the residency at The Thurston. 'The Skiffle Kings' had moved on to bigger gigs throughout the Midlands including The Florence in Kidderminster, where the indominitable Miss Southall, the manager, ruled with a rod of iron and a bottle of gin. She confined the jivers to a roped off area where they couldn't do too much damage.

While singing at The Thurston with 'The Saddletramps', Nick had been spotted by Bill Cordle of 'The Skiffle Kings' who recommended him to Roger Jackson, who was playing piano for 'The Zodiacs' at the time. They were looking for a singer, and Nick jumped at the chance of joining a semi-pro outfit. 'The Zodiacs', formed in 1957 as a skiffle group were, by 1959 a fully fledged rock 'n' roll band, with a pianist adding that extra touch of class.

One day, walking through town, drummer Roger 'Butch' Bowen had spotted Roger Jackson preaching for the Elim Evangelical Church, on the steps of Kidderminster retail market. Butch had heard of Roger Jackson, and approached him to join 'The Zodiacs.'

Roger Jackson was a talented pianist, tall, dark and handsome, ex Coldstream Guards. He had won a talent contest at The Playhouse, playing numbers by Russ Conway, to whom he looked quite similar. Roger agreed to join and was given a piano by Keith Hubbard's mother, and this was the line-up that Nick Miller joined. It didn't last long. Roger Jackson left shortly after to start up on his own. Nick stayed on with 'The Zodiacs' for another nine months until, while shopping in Kidderminster with his girlfriend Audrey, he was approached by Roger Jackson. Roger asked if he would like to join him and his brother Tim, a drummer; they had a residency at The Fountain with plans for a move to London. Once again Nick readily agreed, 'The Zodiacs' were running out of steam as bands do.

So Roger Jackson became Roger Lavern, Nick Miller became Nick Charles and with Tim Jackson on drums, 'The Roger Lavern Combo' was born.

The residency at The Fountain was a great success, they were packing the hall three or four nights a week from April to Christmas 1961. Nick came up with the idea of fitting a Clavioline to the side of the piano, an idea he had borrowed from a Stourport pianist David Floyd. This gave the piano an organ like sound, Roger was not keen on the addition which was quite ironic considering the huge impact it would have on his later life. One regular visitor to The Fountain was a very young Stan Webb who played guitar in one of Roger Lavern's groups during 1960; Stan went on to co-found the famous British blues band 'Chicken Shack'.

During this period Roger Lavern had been making trips to London and had made friends with Ralph Papworth, manager of Walthamstow Granada. He managed to get a booking for the combo supporting 'Marion & The Dicers,' on the Friday night, followed by Roger playing support to Bobby Vee, Clarence 'Frogman' Henry and 'Peter Jay and the Jaywalkers' on the Saturday night. Also at this time, Nick bumped into the famous American pop singer Del Shannon, drinking rye whiskey in the pub opposite the Granada. Nick joined him and cemented a friendship which lasted over 30 years. By a strange coincidence Nick found out some time later that the singer of 'Runaway' had made frinds with Jeff Lynne of ELO who had a home near Pensax in Worcestershire.

So, the die was cast for the move to London and they played an emotional farewell gig at The Fountain on Saturday December 21st. The landlord, Gordon Allard, definitely did not want them to go, they were far to good for business.

Christmas and New Year's Eve passed when, on the eve of their departure, Nick's mum answered a knock on the front door. When she went to answer, she found a bible on the doorstep with a note inside saying, 'God forgive you for sending your lovely son to the wicked city'.

But go they did, driving down to London in one of the worst winters anyone can remember. The snow was falling heavily when Frank Aspey, driver and good friend, drove down the newly constructed M1. The journey should have been quick, but road conditions were appalling, only one lane was open, with snowdrifts twelve foot high on either side; it took them ten hours before they reached 11 Stanhope Road, Highgate. After having a cup of tea, Frank Aspey got straight back in the car and headed for Kidderminster.

Times were hard, they had very little money in spite of Ralph Papworth getting them work around the south east; transport was always a problem. So while Roger returned to Kidderminster to get a motor, Nick managed to set up a meeting with music publishers Noel Gay, after accidently on purpose bumping into Clarence Falconer, one of their top men in a café in Denmark Street, better known as 'Tin Pan Alley.' Roger returned amazingly with a van. The meeting with the publishers went well, but nothing came of it.

Eventually, Roger Lavern got a job through an ad in the music press, for independent record producer RGM. The producer was the legendary Joe Meek, the band ' The Tornados'. This was the final straw for Nick. Totally devastated he headed back home to his parents in Bewdley.

Thereafter, his life took many twists and turns, playing in local bands and working in various sales jobs around the country. He graduated into cabaret, singing at one time with 'The Billy Reid Orchestra.' On one occasion while performing at Cliveden Hall, Lord Astor's country home, he met the famous Christine Keeler, according to Nick, one of the most beautiful women he had ever met. Unfortunately Nick, who had always been a heavy drinker became an alcoholic, living rough on the streets of London; he nearly died in a derelict house in Spitalfields in Londons East End. This became a turning point in Nick's life. He managed to cure himself and went on to found the Chaucer Clinic, an alcohol rehabilitation centre, giving help to people with alcohol problems, including twenty seven professional footballers. In 1997 he was awarded the MBE in the New Year's honours list for, "services to people with alcohol problems". He has written a book about his amazing life entitled, 'Through A Glass Brightly'.

Meanwhile back in London, Roger Lavern was working with his new outfit 'The Tornados'. Formed by Joe Meek, they were used by him to back singers like John Leyton and Billy Fury in his recording studio above a leather shop in the Holloway Road, curiously only a fifteen minute walk away from 11 Stanhope Road, Highgate, the flat where Roger and Nick had moved in to so hopefully only a few months before. The other band members were ex 'Johnny Kidd and the Pirates' Clem Cattini and Alan Caddy, drums and lead respectively, with George Bellamy on rhythm and Heinz Burt on bass. 'The Tornados' became Billy Fury's backing band for live shows as well.

It was during a summer season in August 1962 in Great Yarmouth backing Billy Fury, that the band were called back to London to record a haunting instrumental composed by Joe Meek called *'Telstar'*, named after a recently launched communications satellite.

The recording was done very quickly as the band had to rush back to Great Yarmouth for their evening show. So after they finished laying down their tracks they left Geoff Goddard and Joe Meek to finish the production and sprinkle a little fairy dust. The rest, as they say, is history. *'Telstar'* hit number one in the UK in October 1962 and became number one in the USA in December of the same year. They were the first ever British group to top the American charts. The single sold five million copies worldwide. During this hectic period, Roger managed to squeeze in a visit home in October, to help launch a new range of carpets for Carpet Trades; one of the designs was named Telstar in his honour.

THE TORNADOS *

Further hits followed, although Heinz left the band in January 1963. Always Joe Meek's favourite, he was groomed for stardom and later on had a huge hit with a tribute to Eddie Cochran called, *'Just like Eddie'*; a Geoff Goddard composition.

An American tour was planned for 1963 but unfortunately fell through because Larry Parnes, manager of Billy Fury, vetoed the tour as he feared 'The Tornados' might overshadow his act.

In April 1963 Roger Lavern spent a week in hospital in Kidderminster suffering from exhaustion due to excessive touring. Rumours started to fly that Roger was leaving 'The Tornados'. He wrote a letter to the local press denying that he was leaving the group and that he was shortly off to Paris with 'The Tornados' headlining at The Olympia along with Little Eva of *'Locomotion'* fame. At the end of April they were doing Thank Your Lucky Stars with Billy Fury and another summer season at Great Yarmouth was booked in.

Eventually however the touring got too much and Roger left the group in August 1963. His fifteen months with the group had reportedly earnt him £16,000. He was also said to have received thousands of letters from concerned fans worried about his future. Roger carried on doing cabaret work at Great Yarmouth and then set about forming his own group 'The Microns'.Unusually for the times the band had a female rhythm guitarist, a girl from Hawaii called Trinta. In December he returned to Kidderminster to audition bass players for the new group at The Fountain Inn at Habberley. No one turned up in spite of an offer of fifty pounds per week and a five-year contract, as Roger said at the time "a sad state of affairs indeed". He completed the line up of the group in London and a single self-penned composition '*Christmas Stocking*' was released by Decca in December 1963. It was not a big hit and 'The Microns' eventually split up. Since then Roger has pursued a long and successful career in solo and session work. He was ill for some time but has since recovered and is still playing and recording.

In September 1987, Roger returned to Kidderminster as part of a sixties tribute week organised by local DJ and agent Brian Davies. He appeared at The Fountain, as he stood on stage that evening signing copies of '*Telstar*' his mind must surely have wandered back twenty six years to 1961 when together with his brother Tim and Nick Charles, they played together on the very same stage, packing the audiences in night after night as 'The Roger Lavern Combo'.

And myself, what was I doing all this time? Born on Christmas Eve 1944, nine days after Nick Charles, although our paths never crossed I probably saw him playing with 'The Zodiacs' at the upstairs room at The Hope & Anchor in Stourport. He was going out with the landlord's daughter at the time, a girl I greatly admired although I never said anything more to her than "A pint of mild please". My father was a carpet designer from Glasgow, he moved to Kidderminster for work; almost everything in Kidderminster is connected with carpets. Mum, a nurse from Cardiff, met my father during the war of course; I had one younger brother, Malcolm. Happy childhood till I was 13, when dad died of cancer at the age of 50, probably due to his long term habit of smoking 50/60 cigarettes a day. Dad dying just as my hormones kicked in at the age of thirteen was not a happy combination and I think I must have been a sullen and solitary kid. My one great interest was rock 'n' roll and pop records, spending many hours around the record stall in the indoor market or upstairs at Ronald Wilson's music and record shop, listening to all the latest singles. Mum thought I was a problem, luminous socks, drainpipe trousers and teddy boy quiff. I'd also started drinking. What to do with the boy. Mum had a brother-in-law with connections in the Merchant Navy, as national service had been abolished, this was the second best thing. So I signed up as an apprentice naval cadet, to make a man of me. In January 1961 I found myself heading through Dartmoor on my way, to join the MV 'Blyth Adventurer' docked in Falmouth harbour.

John Combe taken for British Seamans Passport. December 1960

This sojourn on the seven seas lasted about eighteen months, and I visited a lot of places and did things men do in various exotic locations around the world like Curacao, Yokohama, Liberia and Venezuela. In spite of this exciting life on the ocean waves, I did eventually become homesick, and the summer of 1962 found me back in Kidderminster. My first job was with local auctioneers and estate agents, G. Herbert Banks, as a clerk. This turned out to be a more agricultural job than I had anticipated, and after about a year of hauling calves out of trailers, and hens out of pens at the recently opened Kidderminster cattle market (knocked down in 1999), I decided enough was enough and changed jobs. I moved over to becoming a stock records clerk for Carpet Trades, at their brand new office block in Mill Street. This was also knocked down a few years ago; they like knocking things down in Kidderminster! There on the top floor I began talking to fellow clerk Colin Youngjohns about music and was interested to hear that he sang in a local band.

THE GROUPS 1956 - 1962

IN THE BEGINNING

THE BLUE FOUR - THE ROGER LAVERN COMBO

THE CADILLACS-THE GAMBLERS

THE CLIPPERS

THE CRESTAS

THE DANVILLE SAINTS - THE VICTORS

THE INVADERS

NICK MILLER AND THE GRIFFONS

THE ROLLING STONES

THE SADDLETRAMPS

THE SCEPTRES

THE SEVERN VALLEY SKIFFLE KINGS - THE
ROCKIN CASANOVAS

THE CASANOVAS

THE TORNADOS

THE VAMPIRES

PETER WYNNE

THE ZODIACS

IN THE BEGINNING

There was a lively dance band scene in Kidderminster before the arrival of rock 'n' roll. Throughout the 1940s, including the war years, there was live music on Monday, Wednesday, Friday and Saturday nights at The Florence in Blackwell Street, then known as The Gliderdrome, as it had also acted as a roller skating rink. Hundreds of people used to turn up on dance nights. Trumpeter Johnny Rogers joined the Phil Cooper band in 1941, a ten-piece band with a great singer Beryl Turner. Johnny recalls nights at The Gliderdrome when American military bandsmen who were stationed near Kidderminster turned up with their instruments and asked if they could play. After a brief audition in the dressing rooms, they came on stage

THE PHIL COOPER BAND
at the Florence 1946

for a few numbers; they were inevitably excellent musicians.Johnny joined the Marines in 1942 and spent the war in the Far East; there wasn't much time for trumpet playing. He rejoined Phil Cooper in 1946 at The Florence, as it had by now been renamed. However Phil Cooper fell out with the manager Miss Southall in 1947 and the band left the venue.

Johnny Rogers then joined the five-piece 'Tempo Group', who lasted for twenty years. They supported many of the big bands of the era such as Ted Heath, Joe Loss, Edmundo Ross and Ivy Benson at Kidderminster Baths which, during the winter months, was covered over for dancing on Saturday nights. In February 1956 'The Tempo Group' were on stage playing as warm up band to the Joe Loss Orchestra. Johnny heard tinkling noises behind him getting louder and louder until the whole orchestra had joined in with them. It was one of those magical moments.

A fortnight later a film appeared at The Central entitled 'Blackboard Jungle', starring Glenn Ford. A film about delinquent teenagers in New York, it featured in the closing soundtrack the number '*Rock Around The Clock*' by Bill Haley and his Comets.

This was the start of things to come. The film '*Rock Around The Clock*' hit the town in November 1956 and had a huge impact. The dance bands were by no means finished and carried on for quite a few years, however from 1957 onwards rock 'n' roll was definitely on its way, while the dance bands dominance slowly declined.

THE TEMPO GROUP

left to right:
Cliff Smith - drums
Brian Tanner - bass
Roly Haywood - piano
Alan Jones - tenor sax and clarinet
Johnny Rogers - trumpet
at Hartlebury Parish Hall

THE BLUE FOUR
1960 – 1961

This group was formed by Roger Jackson sometime in 1960 before he changed his name to Roger Lavern. With Roger on piano the other members were his brother Tim on drums, Mick Davies on vocals and a very young Stan Webb on guitar. They were supplemented by three girl backing vocalists, the Rowberry sisters from Wolverley.

Based at the Fountain, Roger took on the stage name Lavern in the spring of 1961 with a new line up of brother Tim on drums and Nick Miller, now Nick Charles, on guitar and vocals, they became the 'Roger Lavern Combo' still based mainly at the Fountain. The trio moved to London in January 1962 where they had little success and Nick and Tim returned home. However Roger's luck changed when he joined 'The Tornados' in February 1962.

THE FOUNTAIN INN, LOWER HABBERLEY
Roger Lavern had a successful residency here before he moved to London. Later, Cliff Ward and the Cruisers and the Zodiacs also appeared at the Fountain. Over the years there were many gigs here until 1999 when The Fountain finally succumbed to property developers. The building is still standing but is now converted to residential accommodation.

THE CADILLACS

1957 – 1963

THE CADILLACS (1962)

left to right:
Mick Watkins
David Weale
Ray Swift
Jimmy Mooney
John Wainwright
Ken Chatterton
'Kneeling' Terry Davies
at St. Mary's Hall
Kidderminster
Photo courtesy of John
Wainwright

'The Cadillacs' were formed out of two skiffle groups sometime in the autumn of 1957 with Jimmy Mooney on guitar, Ken Chatterton on bass, Paul Vale on vocals and Maxie Miller on drums. They rehearsed at St. Andrew's Mission Church in Anchorfields, a building long since knocked down when the ring road was built in the 1960s. They eventually got in Ray Swift on drums. Ray had played jazz and was an experienced drummer so Maxie moved onto rhythm guitar.

Their first gig was at The Victoria Club in Pump Street, some time late in 1958, when they asked the main act 'The Danville Saints', if they could do a few numbers. They had their instruments ready and kicked off their first ever gig with Cliff Richards' *'Move It'*.

Later on in 1958 they took third place in Lesley Gold's talent contest at The Playhouse. This led to a matinee and evening performance, their first ever in front of a sit down 'theatre' audience, so they invested in a set of maroon jackets, which they kept throughout their career.

They acquired a manager in Dave 'Spider' Smith, and regular gigs followed at Kidderminster Baths, St. Mary's Hall and Brierley Hill Town Hall, the latter gig being particularly well paid for those days at £13 for the night. On one occasion there they supported the legendary 'Johnny Kidd and The Pirates'.

In 1959 they saw personnel changes, they added alto and tenor sax, Mick Watkins and Dave Weale respectively. Paul Vale left and Terry Davies from Studley took over on vocals. This was the classic 'Cadillacs' line up, which lasted until 1962.

In the summer of 1962, the band hired the town hall and put themselves on with Al Boden's band playing support. After they had paid for the hall, a policeman and a couple of bouncers and a cloakroom attendant, they still came out with £50 in their pocket, after charging 2/6d (12 p) admission.

This gives some idea how many people 'The Cadillacs' could attract in those days. Shortly after this gig Maxie Miller, was replaced by John Wainwright on rhythm guitar. He remembers in June 1962 doing a gig at St. Marys Hall, when new band 'Cliff Ward and The Cruisers' were on the same bill. 'The Cadillacs' had done their set and were waiting to see this new band on the scene, before nipping down to the local boozer. They had to wait sometime, as Cliff Ward had stage fright; this nervousness was to dog him throughout his subsequent career.

Later on in the autumn of 1962 Terry Davies left the band and was replaced on vocals by Tony 'Topsy' Smith. This was the line up when 'The Cadillacs' appeared at Old Hill Plaza in 'November 1962, on the same bill were 'The Beatles' who had just charted with '*Love Me Do*'; Ma Regan's commercial instinct had triumphed again. Also in November 1962, while they were playing the New Meeting Hall, Roger Lavern and Heinz walked in. Heinz was very interested in Ken Chatterton's home made bass guitar and offered good money for it ('*Telstar*' had just hit number one), the answer was in the negative.

Sometime during this period the manager changed from Dave Smith to Calvin Tarpey. However, early 1963 saw 'The Cadillacs' career draw to a close. The beat boom had started, rock 'n' roll began to become old hat. Maxie Miller rejoined for a bit replacing Johnny Wainwright on rhythm, this was proved to be short lived as Ken Chatterton also left. They both joined up with former vocalist Terry Davies with Roger Bayliss on rhythm guitar and Gadgy Philpotts on drums (ex 'Rockin' Casanovas'). This band was called 'The Gamblers' (1963). They only lasted till the end of the year, when they split up due to   musical differences. Ken Chatterton joined 'The Zodiacs' early in 1964 while John Wainwright sold his guitar and amp to pay for a trip to Nashville. Joining a party of 32 country enthusiasts, they were the first British fans to cross 'the pond'. They flew to New York (Idlewild airport for £79 return). They took the Greyhound bus to Nashville, stopping off at Jimmy Skinner's famous record store in Cincinnati. They spent ten days in Nashville, during which time John managed to obtain Jerry Lee Lewis' autograph when he spotted him after a show in Nashville's Municipal Auditorium.

THE GAMBLERS (1963)

left to right:
John Wainwright
'Gadgy' Philpotts
Terry Davies
Ken Chatterton
at Wolverley Memorial Hall.
Photo courtesy of John
Wainwright

THE CLIPPERS

1958 – 1967

THE CLIPPERS
at Brintons Club.
Dave Cartwright on
vocals.

'The Clippers' evolved from a skiffle group called 'The Six Princes' based at the Prince of Wales pub in Hagley. Original members Anthony Smith and Maurice Reeves were joined by Vic Rose on drums from 'The Severn Valley Skiffle Kings'. Vic replaced washboard player Brian Mann, who then became their manager.

Maurice, Brian and Vic met when they worked together at Brintons. They were then joined by Bruce McCreddie on lead guitar and Ron Horton, singer, who was a drinking partner of Vic's. With Anthony on bass and Maurice on rhythm, they became 'The Clippers', named after Bruce's motorbike a Royal Enfield 'Clipper'.

Most of their practising was done in Vic's parents front room in Lorne Street, Kidderminster, with the only amp they possessed plugged into the light socket. They were now ready to rock 'n' roll.

Early bookings for the band were The Swan at Chaddesley and The Swan at Wychbold where Bruce thought up the idea of the Clippers Rock 'n' Roll Club, the band having the first five membership cards; it was a great success until the brewery clamped down on the idea and the gig finished. Other early venues were The Mare and Colt and Brintons Club.

When Ron had to leave in 1959 to do his national service, Dave Cartwright from Stourbridge was drafted in on vocals, which he did for two years. When Ron came back they carried on with the two singers, Dave on the more melodic numbers, Ron on the rockier ones. One of the regular venues during this period was The Wharf at Holt Fleet. Run by the legendary Jim Quinn it was a good gig for 'The Clippers' where they increased their membership in spite of the occasional punch up and a freezing cold dance hall in the winter. There was an open fire in the room. Lit by Jim it generated no heat but vast clouds of smoke, which watered the eyes and irritated Ron Horton's already well strained vocal chords. Another good venue for the band was The Park Attwood, set in its own grounds in Trimpley. They played there on Thursdays and Saturdays alternating with 'Cliff Ward and the Cruisers' and 'Tommy and The Crestas' and other bands of the era.

During 1962/1963 Vic left the band because of work commitments and the drummers seat was taken over by Ray Weston from Lapworth, whose brother Graham later on became manager of the group. Graham was an actor in the famous TV soap Crossroads at the time. In January 1962 during the time with the two singers they entered a rock 'n' roll contest at Handsworth Plaza. They won their semi–final, Joe Brown was the judge on the night. Dave Cartwright had suggested doing Cliff Richard's *The Young Ones*. Bruce turned the idea down flat. 'The Clippers' were rock 'n' rollers; no soft numbers thank you, so it was Eddie Cochran's *Somethin Else*.

Bruce was right, every other band had chosen *The Young Ones* as their number but in the finals they came third. Bert Weedon was the judge this time. He said the band lacked continuity, they were a bit raw for Bert's taste. Adam Faith presented the prizes but the band didn't turn up for the prize-giving, third place was not for them, so their manager at the time Chris Smart from Hagley picked it up on their behalf.

Around this time Dave Cartwright left the group to follow a solo career as a singer-songwriter, and went on to release 5 LPs of his own songs during the folk-boom of the 70s.

'The Clippers' were probably the first local group to play abroad, following a holiday on the Costa Brava in 1962. Bruce and Maurice managed to secure a gig for the band in the Carisco Club in the Hotel Solterra Playa, Lloret de Mar then a relatively unspoilt fishing port. So the following summer of 1963 saw Bruce and Maurice driving to Spain in Bruce's Ford Consul with the bands gear stowed in the boat on the trailer.

THE CLIPPERS
left to right:
Bruce McCreddie
Maurice Reeve
Anthony Smith
Vic Rose
Ron Horton
Photo taken at Anthony
Smiths wedding 6th June
1964 at the Lickey End
Club, Bromsgrove.

Anthony arrived a couple of days later at Barcelona airport, his flight had been delayed which was just as well as Bruce and Maurice were also late, being totally wrecked after a tour of the local bars. Bruce then proceeded to drive the Consul the wrong way up the dual carriage way. Fortunately they managed to exit at the first slip road without crashing into anybody.

On drums they took on Rafael a local Spanish drummer who played with the hotel house band, an Italian group with the wonderful name of "Jesus Marino and His Boys". Rafael's main advice to 'The Clippers' was "no propaganda". The band never quite understood this, but assumed it was something to do with Franco.

They played every night for a fortnight, the gig went well and they were offered a winter season in the Canaries and a booking the following summer back on the Costa Brava. Although a tempting offer, both Bruce and Anthony had good jobs so turned the chance down.

In 1964 Vic rejoined the band on drums. It was at this time they made their first recordings at the Hollick and Taylor studios in Birmingham. They first did a demo for an aspiring songwriter and then decided to record six of their own numbers. Time was of the utmost importance as you had to pay studio time from the moment you walked in. Anyway they recorded the six numbers on three demo discs. Bruce took them round the record companies in London with no luck, Norrie Paramor telling Bruce that the numbers were "not in the current idiom". Years later however one of these songs 'Till the day I die' was included in a compilation album 'In the Forest" alongside

Dave Cartwright and many other local artistes.

The groups earthy rock 'n' roll style rock fitted in well with the new beat boom and they filled out halls regularly until they played their final gig at Abberley Village Hall on March 4th 1967. Bruce in particular was getting more interested in his boats than the band.

Nothing much was said on the night, but as Anthony drove home, he knew instinctively that 'The Clippers' would never play again; he was correct.

THE CRESTAS

1959 – 1961

THE CRESTAS
left to right:
Nigel Bache
Nigel Turrall
Alfie Knott
Tim Wilson
Dave Mansfield
Worcester Cross Youth
Club.

'The Crestas' were originally formed in 1959 when singer Alfie Knott discovered a bunch of lads rehearsing skiffle numbers above The Birches pub in Stourport Road, courtesy of the landlord Cyril Smith. This original line up consisted of Bob Barber, Bob McBirnie on tea chest bass and Nigel Turrall on washboard. Nigel's dad bought him a snare drum and a pair of sticks. They had started proper rehearsals at the Worcester Cross Youth Club, and when the two Bobs dropped out, the line up was Alfie Knott – vocals, Tim Wilson – bass, Nigel Turrall – drums, with two strumming guitarists Brian Jones and Brian Hayden. Their first gig was also at the Worcester Cross Youth Club on Tuesday March 15th 1960, when Tim Wilson struck up the bass run to 'Baby I don't care'.

Further gigs followed at Arley Village Hall and Broadwaters Youth Club where they met Nigel Bache who took over on lead guitar. Not long before this the two strumming guitarists had left to be replaced temporarily by

George Harrison on lead guitar, but he didn't stay long, Nigel Bache being a more than adequate replacement.

Their first paid gig was at Stourport Town Hall, where they earned the princely sum of £2 , supporting 'The Zodiacs'. An extremely young Kevyn Gammond played rhythm guitar on the night. He did a few more gigs for them but was soon replaced by Dave Mansfield. This line up of Alfie Knott – vocals, Nigel Bache – lead, Dave Mansfield – rhythm, Tim Wilson – bass, Nigel Turrall – drums, lasted until the end of 1961. In April of that year 'The Crestas' played Frank Freemans, the first rock 'n' roll act to do so.

One Sunday afternoon late in 1961 while rehearsing at the Hope and Anchor in Stourport, Dave Mansfield had a bust up with Alfie Knott, the upshot being that Alfie left the band. A few weeks later while rehearsing at The Bridge Inn, Stourport,   Dave Mansfield introduced a new singer to the group, a young lad called Tommy Noyes, who worked with him at Parsons Chain. Dave said he was singing at work all the time so he ought to do it properly and after a few rehearsals the band went out at the beginning of 1962 as 'Tommy and The Crestas'. They became one of Kidderminster's most popular groups and played regularly in the area for many years to come.

THE DANVILLE SAINTS
1957 – 1959

'The Danvilles' were the second Skiffle band to form in the area. Terry Salters, with a few friends had seen the 'Severn Valley Skiffle Kings' at the Tontine in Stourport. Inspired by them they decided to start up their own Skiffle group in November 1957 at the Worcester Cross Youth Club. The original line up was: Carl Hasdell - electric guitar, Geoff Baker – strumming guitar, John Parry – tea chest bass, Terry Salters – banjo and vocals and Paul Booton – drums. Geoff Baker didn't stay long and was soon replaced by Al Boden – guitar and vocals who had just finished his national service.

Their first gig was at St. John's Parish Hall followed shortly after by the Mare and Colt. By the time they played at a parents' evening at the Worcester Cross Youth Club they had all acquired stage names. They were now known as Carl 'Ike' Hasdell, John 'Cactus' Parry, Terry 'Bullet' Salters, Paul 'Wilbur' Booton and Al 'Hank' Boden.

A Thursday night residency followed at the newly opened Radcliffe Arms on Birchen Coppice, Fred Hunt being the landlord at the time. Terry Salters remembers this gig particularly well as members of the audience used to give him notes with the words of the songs they were doing written on them, as Terry's grasp of the lyrics were a little patchy to put it mildly. A prestige gig for 'The Danvilles' was an appearance at the Playhouse, where they were part of the gang show, and wore for the occasion their newly acquired tartan waistcoats.

Their first away gig was at the Warner's holiday camp at Dovercourt Bay, Harwich where Terry's mother organised holidays for the carpet workers. They also played at the Birmingham Hippodrome doing talent contests for Jim Dale Discoveries and Carrol Levis Discoveries. They got to the final of the latter but didn't do it, as they had honoured a commitment to friends in another band they had met at Harwich, to play at their club in London.

This line up stayed the same until 1960, the band gradually moving away from skiffle to rock 'n' roll, when John Parry left and also Al Boden to do Country and Western music. The transformation was now complete. The new line up was: Terry Salters – vocals and rhythm guitar, Peter Reading – lead guitar, Dave Arnold – bass, Paul Booton – drums, Carl Hasdell – guitar and vibraphones and Tony Owen on piano, which meant the group could add Jerry Lee Lewis numbers to their repertoire. With the new line up came a new name.....

THE DANVILLE SAINTS
at Worcester Cross Youth Club.
November 1957

left to right:
Geoff Baker
Paul Booton
Terry Salters
Carl Hasdell
John Parry

THE VICTORS
1960 – 1964

The band bought the first three Burns guitars imported into the UK, purchasing all three on the same day (on the HP of course) from Jack Woodruffs in Birmingham.

Regular gigs for 'The Victors' were St. Mary's Hall, the Labour Club and a Friday night residency at Jon and Patty's dance studio in Stourport. By this time Roger Jackson had taken over from Tony Owen on piano. When he first joined the band Roger used to keep a white bible on his piano as he was a member of the Elim Evangelical Church at the time. While with 'The Victors', Roger won a talent competition at The Playhouse doing Russ Conway numbers.

Later on, 'The Victors' had a memorable gig at Kidderminster Town Hall supporting 'Screamin' Lord Sutch and The Savages'. 'The Savages' let 'The Victors' use their equipment for their second set.

By 1964 'The Victors' had run out of steam, rock 'n' roll was going out of fashion. Terry Salters was married and heavily involved in local football, and the others dropped out for various reasons. However, Dave Arnold carried on his musical career by joining 'Tommy and The Crestas'.

THE INVADERS
1960 – 1964

'The Invaders' were a Bewdley based band originally called 'El Saint and the Sinners'. They were Bill Sedgeley – guitar and vocals, Dave Millichip – guitar, Mick Dickenson – bass, Dave Tiplady – drums and vocals. The group started off like so many others at Worcester Cross Youth Club. After a while they decided to change their name and whilst browsing through a book on trains they found a locomotive called 'The Invader', a good name for a band, (it made a change from cars anyway). They supported the main acts at Stourbridge and Kidderminster Town Halls. These included 'Screamin' Lord Sutch and The Savages' and Tommy Bruce at Stourbridge, and 'The Spotnicks', 'Brian Poole and The Tremeloes' and 'The Searchers' at Kidderminster.

After 'The Searchers' gig, 'The Invaders' found that their old Bedford van had messages of devotion written all over it in lipstick. Even the support bands got star treatment in those days.

In the Summer of 1964 'The Invaders' had a two month summer season based at 'The Blue Lagoon Club' in Newquay, from where they played halls and clubs all over Cornwall. Unfortunately they were left stranded there by

THE INVADERS
Cornwall, Summer 1964
left to right:
Mick Dickenson - bass, Les Griffiths - guitar (Replaced Dave Millichip)
Bill Sedgley - lead guitar, Dave Tiplady - drums

their agent and had to make their own way home with the help of relatives who were staying nearby. Being somewhat disillusioned by this, they changed management and became involved instead with Worcestershire horse trainers, Martin Tate, Ken Oliver and Richard Arbuthnott (also with the Palethorpe family of sausage fame). They used to hire 'The Invaders' for big society parties where the pay and perks were much better.

Later on Josie Tongue became their manager and her daughter Lorraine joined the band as a vocalist. At this time the group entered talent contests at the Central cinema, Kidderminster and Malvern Winter Gardens and won a trip to appear at the finals in Morecambe. They eventually split up in 1966, when Mick Dickenson joined Butch Humbers 'Huskies'. Bill Sedgeley had a chance to join 'The Eagles' from Bristol but did not take up the offer. Dave Tiplady went semi-pro under the stage name of Dave Mountain.

NICK MILLER & THE GRIFFONS
1962 - 1963

The Group was formed by Nick Miller on his return from London. The line up was Nick Miller – guitar and vocals, Bob Spencer – lead guitar, Alan Minton – bass, Bob Newton – drums. Both Bob Spencer and Bob Newton played with Cliff Ward in his first ever group 'The Senators'. Bob Newton was last heard of making radio jingles in Thailand. Nick went on to form 'The Nick Charles Set' in the mid sixties.

THE ROLLING STONES
1962 - 1963

Don't get excited, this young Kidderminster band formed early in 1962, eventually changed their name when the other group from London had their first hit 'Come On' in the summer of 1963. Brothers Martin and Rob Smith on guitars were joined by Ian Hardiman on bass. Ian had spotted the trio (Ron Griffiths on drums) doing Everly Brothers numbers in a support spot at Frank Freemans. Ian had been playing cello in the County Youth Orchestra but the lure of rock 'n' roll got him to take up the electric bass. With the addition of lead vocalist Bob Bullen, The Rolling Stones did their first gig as support to 'The Zodiacs' at The Fountain in the summer of 1962. The band lasted a year as 'The Rolling Stones', until in the summer of 1963 they dropped their name, their lack of long hair causing confusion amongst some punters. They called themselves from then on 'The Ward Five'.

THE SADDLETRAMPS
1958

A very young Bewdley based skiffle/rock group who took over the 'Severn Valley Skiffle Kings' residency at The Thurston. Nick Miller – rhythm guitar and vocals, Ron Perrin – lead guitar, Nick Faulkner – bass and Graham 'Gadgy' Philpotts – drums. They only lasted a year. Nick Miller joined 'The Zodiacs', while 'Gadgy' Philpotts and Ron Perrin joined 'The Rocking Casanovas'.

THE SCEPTRES
1961

When Colin Youngjohns left school in the Easter of 1961 he started work at Brintons where he met creeler Roy Campbell. They discovered they had a mutual interest in music, so they joined up with Rob Smith – lead guitar, Mick Waldron – rhythm and Phil Moseley on bass, Colin was on vocals and Roy Campbell on drums to from 'The Sceptres'.

Their first gig was as support to 'The Crestas' at Frank Freemans. They had two Watkins Dominator amps which everything went through. They also supported 'The Zodiacs' at Franks. Keith Hubbard of 'The Zodiacs' must have spotted potential in 'The Sceptres' as he asked Colin, Roy and Mick Waldron to join himself and Mick Birch to form 'The Zodiacs' (Mk.2). ' The Sceptres' short career was finished.

THE SEVERN VALLEY SKIFFLE KINGS
1956 - 1959

Formed in the Spring of 1956 'The Skiffle Kings' were the first skiffle group in the area. Vocalist Tony Goodwin had been inspired, by hearing 'Chris Barber's Jazzmen's' rendition of 'Bobby Shaftoe' on Jack Payne's radio show. Tony became a big Chris Barber fan and through him of Lonnie Donegan, who had his own spot with Chris Barber's 'Jazzmen'.

SEVERN VALLEY SKIFFLE KINGS
at the Thurston Hotel, Bewdley

left to right:
Bill Cordle - banjo & vocals
Trevor Edwards - drums & washboards
Ken Beeston - thrash guitar & congas
Tony Goodwin - guitar & vocals
Geoff Goodwin - tea chest bass and later cello bass
Howard Tolley - lead guitar

So Tony and five other friends including brother Geoff formed a six-piece skiffle group, and managed to obtain a residency at The Thurston Hotel in Bewdley.

The band's original equipment was rudimentary in the extreme; a banjo doubled up as a drum skin, a putty tub with a 'shammy' leather over it acted as a conga, together with acoustic guitars and the obligatory washboard and tea chest bass made up the band's equipment. The amplification was one old radio set.

Their material consisted mostly of Lonnie Donegan numbers and obscure Mississippi Delta stuff. The kids loved it, The Thurston was jam-packed for a year. In August 1957 they won their heat of the World Skiffle Group Contest at the Mecca Ballroom, Birmingham. In 1958 they went on to audition for TV impresario Carroll Levis. After their second set, Carroll Levis told them "Great boys, I want you for my show". He meant his stage show at Worcester Gaumont, not his TV show. The band played the shows anyway but eventually split up in 1959 as skiffle faded away and rock 'n' roll took over.

There were a few changes during the three years of 'The Skiffle Kings' existence. Trevor Edwards, left in January 1958 to be replaced by Vic Rose on a proper drum kit, Vic had played with Tony and Geoff Goodwin before when they had a jazz group. He later went on to join 'The Clippers'. Tony Morris replaced Howard Tolley on lead guitar. Geoff Goodwin left in 1959 to return to his first love, jazz. Later on that same year Tony and Bill Cordle joined up with ex-Saddletramps 'Gadgy' Philpotts on drums and Ron Perrins on lead guitar, also joining them was Lenny Harrison on rhythm guitar. They called themselves ....

THE ROCKIN' CASANOVAS
1959 - 1962

'The Rockin' Casanovas' were playing one night at Dudley Roller Rink, a venue with a reputation for the worst teddy boys in the Midlands when the manager gave Tony a starting pistol and told him to fire it in the air if there was any trouble. Nothing happened during their first set, but in the second set Tony got a bit carried away during one of their more raucous numbers and shot in the air. No one turned a 'brylcreemed' head.

In June 1962 rhythm guitarist Lenny Harrison was killed in a car crash near Tenbury Wells. This broke the spirit of the band and they split up. Tony Goodwin and Bill Cordle carried on later in the year as 'The Casanovas', a duo doing 'Everly Brothers' numbers. Bill Cordle eventually emigrated to Canada, where he had some success on Canadian TV and in Toronto night clubs as a ballad singer and also as a film extra. Sadly Bill died on one of his trips home visiting family and friends in June 1980.

THE TORNADOS WITH ROGER LAVERN

April 1962 - August 1963

Roger Lavern left his job as a wages clerk with carpet manufacturers William Hill Limited in the Christmas of 1961.

Moving to London in January 1962, he joined The Tornados in April. The original Tornados line up was:

Alan 'Tea' Caddy - lead guitar
Roger Lavern - keyboards
Clem Cattini - drums
Heinz Burt - bass
George Bellamy - rhythm guitar *

Alan Caddy and Clem Cattini were ex-Johnny Kidd and the Pirates, while Heinz was chosen more for his looks than his musical abilities. They were initially used by Joe Meek as session musicians in his recording studios in the Holloway Road, backing such artists as John Leyton, Ricky Wayne, Don Charles, The Forresters, Gerry Temple and Michael Cox and most importantly Billy Fury. In fact Billy Fury had a name check in 'The Tornados' first single *'Love and Fury'*. They were also Billy's backing band for live shows. 'The Tornados' also toured in their own right in Scotland, Manchester and Coventry and made personal appearances at an International Star Gala in May 1962 to promote their first single. During this time Billy Fury had been in America. On his return they began a fourteen week summer season at The Windmill Theatre, Great Yarmouth as Billy's backing band. It was during this period, in August, that they recorded their second single *'Telstar'*. The record was a sensation. It climbed the charts hitting the number one spot in October 1962, selling a million copies in the UK alone. In December *'Telstar'* reached number one in the US charts and stopped there for three weeks. Total sales eventually reached five million copies. On Saturday the 15th, Billy Fury presented 'The Tornados' with a gold disc on TV for a million sales of the single *'Telstar'*.

A tour of the States had been arranged for February 1963 but was cancelled due to disagreements between Joe Meek and Larry Parnes. Larry was insisting that Billy Fury had to go as well. No amicable agreement was forthcoming and the tour fell through. More hit singles were followed by more tours. By August 1963 Roger Lavern had had enough of the endless touring and left along with George Bellamy and replacement bass player Brian Gregg. Roger, was replaced on keyboards by Jimmy O'Brien. For the purposes of this book the story of 'The Tornados' finishes here, although the band carry on for quite a few years. For those interested in 'The Tornados', Joe Meek and the music of the era, a book written by Joe Repsch first sold in 1989 and entitled 'The Legendary Joe Meek' is a must to get hold of.

LINE UP CHANGES
APRIL 1962 - AUGUST 1963

Jan - 1963
   Heinz Burt leaves to pursue solo career, replaced on bass firstly by Chas Hodges and then Tab Martin.

March 1963
   Tab Martin leaves. Ex-Johnny Kidd and The Pirates, Brian Gregg takes over on bass until Aug 1963.

DISCOGRAPHY (WITH ROGER LAVERN)
Acknowledgment to Record Collector,   March 1997

Decca   F11449 *Love and Fury/Popeye Twist.* April 1962

Decca   F11494   *Telstar/Jungle Fever* (No.1) August 1962
Decca   F11562   *Globetrotter/Locomotion With Me* (no.5)
               Jan 1963
Decca   F11606   *Robot/Life on Venus* (No. 17) March 1963
Decca   F11662   *The Ice Cream Man/Theme from 'The*
               Scales of Justice' (No.18) May 1963
SRT. SRTS.75350   *Telstar/Red Rocket* – 1975

   This was a recording of Telstar by the original Tornados in 1975.
   The best CD compilation is probaly the EP collection 'See For Miles', SEECD 445 released in 1996.

EP's

Decca DFE 8510   *The Sounds of The Tornados*
      (No.2) October 1962
Decca DFE 8511   *Telstar* (No.4) November 1962
Decca DFE 8521   *More Sounds from 'The Tornados'*
      (No.9) March 1963
Decca DFE 8533   *Tornados Rock* (No.7) July 1963

Sheet music to the sounds of the
Tornados EP released Oct. 1962 *

LP's

Decca LK4524   'Just For Fun' a film soundtrack includes "*All the Stars in the Sky*" by The Tornados.

Over the years many compilations by 'The Tornados' have been released, some with Roger Lavern on keyboards. An LP entitled '*Telstar*' was released in America only and charted there in February 1963 at number 45. In 1994 after many years of legal battles the group releases the LP – *Telstar* – the original sixties hits of 'The Tornados', on the 'Music Collection International' label.

ROGER LAVERN – SINGLES

Decca F11791 –   *Christmas Stocking/Reindeer Ride* – Dec 1963. With his new group 'The Microns'.

SRT. SRTS/CUS.402. Sing-a-long Piano Party Parts 1&2 (Maxi Single 1975)

REUNIONS

In May 1991 the original Tornados played a tribute concert to Joe Meek at the Lewisham Theatre, London. Other acts performing on the night were, 'Screamin' Lord Sutch', Cliff Bennett, The Honeycombs, Mike Berry, Heinz, The Moontrekkers and Danny Rivers.

POSTCRIPT

In February 1967 Joe Meek committed suicide, after first killing his landlady, at 304 Holloway Road, with a shotgun belonging to Heinz. This was a tragic end to a life tormented by his sexuality. He was an innovative and eccentric record producer, a pioneer of pop music production in the early 1960s. Heinz Burt died on 17th April 2000. He had a Kidderminster connection as he often visited the carpet town with fellow Tornado Roger Lavern. He had one great hit *"Just Like Eddie"* written by Geoff Goddard who died a month after Heinz on the 15th May 2000. The year 2000 was not a good year for The Tornados; Alan Caddy died on the 16th of August of the same year.

Acknowledgements on 'The Tornados' to Spencer Leigh.

THE VAMPIRES
1960 - 1962

'The Vampires' grew out of a skiffle/country trio 'The Johnny Rebs' with Ray Percy on drums and vocals, Graham Drew and John Wainwright on guitars. They were joined by Trevor Jones on bass and temporarily Gerry Murphy on vocals. Gerry didn't stay long, they took on a mysterious dark haired drummer from Bradford, with Ray Percy taking over the vocals. The drummer from Bradford gave them their name 'The Vampires' and supplied small cloth bats which they ironed on their shirts. One night during a gig at the Walshes Tenants Hall, Graham Drew was approached by Cliff Ward to join a band he was forming, Graham was keen and left 'The Vampires' to join 'The Cruisers'. Shortly afterwards John Wainwright was asked by Ray Swift, drummer with 'The Cadillacs', if he'd like to join them, to replace Maxie Miller on guitar. John agreed, 'The Vampires' were no more.

THE VAMPIRES
left to right
Graham Drew
Ray Percy
John Wainwrigght.
Photo courtesy of
John Wainwright

34

PETER WYNNE

Peter Wynne or Peter Hazelwood as he was known then, started off his career in 1956 at the age of seventeen singing a few numbers with the resident band of 'The Black Horse' – The Carlton Orchestra. He had had jobs as a laboratory assistant in a carpet firm, as a police cadet and a spell in the Grenadier Guards. After leaving the Army, Peter was encouraged by friends to turn professional, so early in 1959 he moved to London to try his hand as a full-time singer.

Peter auditioned with Oscar Rabin and Eric Winstone and was unlucky not to get work with them. Eventually he appeared on the radio version of 'Opportunity Knocks' with Hughie Green. Impressed by the young singer, Hughie rang up Norman Newell at EMI and got Peter to sing down the telephone. Suitably impressed, Norman invited Peter to audition for him at EMI's Chappell Studios. Russ Conway played piano on the audition. Peter passed and was given a four single contract on the Parlophone Label. His first single, *'Twilight Time'* (the Platters number) on the B-side (with backing by Geoff Love and his orchestra). At this time Peter was holding down a day job as a commis chef at the Victoria Club in Edgeware Road. He also worked at Lyons Corner House, at Marble Arch and it was there while pushing a tray of cakes up to the counter, singing away as usual, that he met Larry Parnes' mum. Impressed by Peter's voice, she told Larry about him. Larry Parnes sent his assistant Hal Carter to the Corner House to check him out. Hal thought he had potential so Peter auditioned for Larry Parnes. Larry liked what he heard and signed Peter up to his stable of artists who included Billy Fury, Marty Wilde and fellow ballad singer Johnny Gentle amongst many others. In fact Peter inherited Marty Wilde's silver lamè suit, which he then used as his stage gear. It was at this time that Peter changed his surname to Wynne, after his uncle Furness Wynne Williams, an opera singer with D'Oyle Carte. One of Larry Parnes' ideas was to send Peter to Italy to train as an opera singer and to change his name to Pedro. For some reason this never came off and Peter commenced his professional career as Peter Wynne.

Larry Parnes' power as a manager was soon evident, appearances in the spring and summer of 1960 in Jack Good's TV show 'Boy Meets Girl' hosted by Marty Wilde was a follow up to the famous 'Oh Boy'. Peter appeared on the show four times doing cover versions like *'Wild One'* and *'Way Down Yonder In New Orleans'*. Further TV appearances followed in Jack Good's next pop programme 'Wham'.

Early in 1960 Peter was added to the 'Anglo-American Rock Show', a package tour which had started in January starring American rock performers Eddie Cochran and Gene Vincent and British artists like Duffy Power, Johnny Gentle and a very young (16 years old) Georgie Fame, playing with Colin Green and the Beat Boys. At the time, Georgie had his own solo spot at the start at the second set. When Gene Vincent dropped out through illness at the Manchester gig, Peter was flown up to help bolster the number of singers on the show. He was totally amazed to find that as he walked out on stage he was confronted by thousands of teenage girls screaming at him. The following day in the write up in the Daily Express, Peter's singing was described as the 'Golden Voice of the Sixties'. He was kept on for the rest of the tour. The last show was at the Bristol Hippodrome on April 16th, but a second leg was booked to start in May, as the tour had been so successful.

Before Eddie Cochran left for a two-week break in the States, in his usual friendly manner he asked if anybody would like anything bought back for them. Peter asked for a pair of authentic American jeans "Sure thing man, no problem", was Eddie's reply. Everybody parted company. Eddie, together with his girlfriend Sharon Sheeley and Gene Vincent, hired a taxi to take them to London Airport. Peter together with fellow singer Johnny Gentle set off shortly after in their own car also heading back to London. As they were approaching Chippenham on the A4 they noticed they were running out of petrol and seeing a policeman they stopped and asked him where the nearest garage was. The policeman said there had been an accident just down the road; a taxi had crashed. If they got there quickly they might be able to siphon some petrol out, but by the time they reached the spot, everything had been cleared. Thinking little more about it, they eventually got some petrol and carried on to London.

The following day when Peter heard the news on the radio that Eddie Cochran had been in the crash just outside Chippenham the previous night, he was totally devastated. In spite of Eddie Cochran's death the second leg of the tour went ahead, Eddie Cochran's name being rather unceremoniously crossed off the poster for the gig at Liverpool Stadium on May 30th. It was at this gig that Peter met The Beatles when they introduced themselves backstage. Peter didn't take much notice at the time, but George Harrison kept in touch for a while afterwards.

Gene Vincent, always a heavy drinker, missed the steady influence of Eddie Cochran on the road and really hit the bottle. On one occasion on the tour bus he threatened Peter with a large knife he owned which he gave the pet name 'Henry', when Peter had the temerity to tell Gene to quieten down late one night on the way home from a gig. The following day, Gene had calmed down, apologised to Peter and offered him a swig of his Canadian Club Whiskey.

Another package tour followed in the Autumn of 1960. 'The Rock 'n' Trad' spectacular starred Billy Fury, Joe Brown, Tommy Bruce, Peter Wynne and various other pop and jazz acts. Peter remembers the Glasgow Empire particularly well, because towards the end of Billy's first set, brass ashtrays from the back of the theatre seats began flying through the air towards the stage, some of the men in the audience taking exception to Billy's popularity with the girls. One hit the cymbals, causing the drummer Red Rees to leave the stage, followed shortly by other members of the band. Billy struggled on valiantly but had to give up in the end as ashtrays flew around him. Peter wanted to go on and do his set but he was told not to perform; the show was abandoned and the artists had to wait one and a half hours before leaving the building.

Life on the road could certainly be dangerous at times. On another occasion Peter and Ricky Valance had a lucky escape when the car they were travelling in spun off the road on the way back from a Scottish gig. Ricky Valance had cuts and bruises but Peter needed stitches. Ironically Ricky Valance's hit single "*Tell Laura I Love Her*", all about a car crash, was in the charts at the time.

Peter Wynne had four singles released by Parlophone. The last single, "*The Wall*", had TV promotion on "Thank Your Lucky Stars", but like the other three singles it failed to chart. Rock 'n' Roll had made it difficult for ballad singers like Peter. However, cover versions of American hit singles like '*Twilight Time*' or '*It's Only Make Believe*' which Peter had recorded as B-sides, would probably have been more successful.

During all this time Peter had regular live work thanks to Larry Parnes. Now Simon Smith, he does a summer season with Lonnie Donegan at 'The Brittania' Great Yarmouth, followed the next year by a season at Blackpool. This proved too much for Peter (Simon). His patience with Larry Parnes came to an end. Larry had an idea that all his artists should dress up as ATS girls for a comedy act. Peter protested but was told in no uncertain terms to take part or leave the show. He did it once, but told Larry that his main ballad singer shouldn't be doing comedy sketches and left. This was the last time Peter worked with Larry Parnes. Although a hard taskmaster and shrewd, especially about money, Peter remembers Larry Parnes as generous at times and always kept his acts on retainers of £35 a week, not a bad wage for the early 60s.

MAY 1960

JACARANDA ENTERPRISES
. . . . BY ARRANGEMENT WITH LARRY PARNES

THE GREATEST SHOW EVER TO BE STAGED

LIVERPOOL STADIUM
Tuesday, May 3rd at 8 p.m.
(THREE HOUR PROGRAMME)

BY SENSATIONAL DEMAND   RETURN OF
Gene Vincent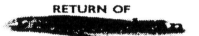

Sensational Added Attraction from U. S. A.
Davy Jones
ITALY'S NERO AND HIS GLADIATORS

Peter Wynne   Lance Fortune

The Viscounts

Colin Green   Billy Raymond
AND THE BEAT BOYS   YOUR HOST & COMPERE

PLUS Liverpool's CASS AND THE CASSANOVAS
RORY STORM AND THE HURRICANES
& OTHER LEADING LIVERPOOL ROCK GROUPS

PRICES: — 10/- — 7/6d. — 5/- — 3/6d.
Tickets available from Lewis's, Cranes, Rushworth's, Beaver Radio, Frank
Hessy,, The Stadium, Top Hat Record Bar, Dale St.,
and the Jacaranda Coffee Bar.

*Poster of Liverpool Stadium
show, note Eddie Cochrans'
name crossed out*

Working now as Simon Smith, Peter did plenty of live work back at Great Yarmouth the following summer with Vince Eager, Tommy Bruce and old mate Johnny Gentle, followed by pantomime at 'The London Palladium' as understudy to Frank Ifield in 'Babes in the Wood'. This was followed by a tour with the musical 'Camelot' and a new single released on Columbia in 1966 – "*This Is My Beloved*".

Publicity photo of Peter taken in Regents Park by EMI to promote name change to Simon Smith

After 'Camelot', a residency followed at the prestigious Stork Club with Larry Grayson, in Londons West End, and another summer season at Lowestoft with 'The Rockin Berries'.

In 1969 Peter changed direction and moved to the States. Living in Miami he had a residency at The Fontainbleau Hotel, a prestigious venue where Frank Sinatra had sung previously. During his time there he flew to Nashville and recorded a single *'The Hole That Holds the Bones'*. He also did a live show for the Nashville Convention, which was broadcast on TV in the States and Canada. He sang "*It's Only Make Believe*" and the B-side of his single *'My Kind of Love'* written by guitarist Jerry Reed. The live theatre audience gave Peter a great response, which created a lot of interest at the Convention. Dick Broderick head of the Country and Western Association based in New York took over negotiations for Peter. Capitol Records in particular were very interested but arguments over advances and whether Peter should sing country or not blocked a deal and the whole thing fell through. Back in Miami, Peter's agent had managed to set him up a spot on the Johnny Carson TV show, at that time the number one music show in the States, broadcast from coast to coast. So Peter flew to New York from Miami in the winter of 1970. Dressed in his normal Florida gear of slacks and short sleeve shirts, Peter hadn't bargained for a freezing New York winter. A severe cold and sore throat followed and the TV appearance was cancelled. He did carry on for a while longer at 'The Fontainbleau' and also another top venue 'The Diplomat', however all the disappointments had made Peter disillusioned and in 1971 he returned to Cardiff where he carried on doing the clubs around the UK.

He eventually returned to Stourport in 1993. Sitting in The Brintons Arms one night he got talking to Nigel Bache from 'The Crestas' who said they needed a singer as Tommy Noyes had just left. So Peter joined 'The Crestas'. Dave Mansfield – rhythm guitarist, remembered seeing Peter playing the part of Will Scarlett at the London Palladium, way back in 1966.

Peter sang with 'The Crestas' for a couple of years, until he had to retire with throat problems. In a way Peter's life has turned full circle from Kidderminster to London and the States and then back home again.

DISCOGRAPHY

Chapel of Love (Myles) / *Twilight Time*
      (M & A Nevins, Dunn)
      With Geoff Love and his Orchestra.
      Parlophone – R4597 – 1959.

Ask Anyone In Love (Shapiro, Lynn) / *I Need You Close Again*
      (Firmstone, Williams & Barratt)
      Parlophone – R4668 – 1960.

Our Concerto / *Your Love*
      Parlophone 1961.

The Wall (Williams, Firmstone) / *You're Mine* (Wynne)
      Parlophone – R4884 – 1962.

I'm A Fool To Want You (F Sinatra, J Woolf, J Herron) / *It's A*
      Lonely Town (Pomus / Shuman)
      Recorded in Hamburg.
      Polydor 52316 – 1964.

This Is My Beloved / *I Just Can't Live Without You* (Smith)
      Columbia 1966.
The Hole That Holds The Bones (Koch, Wilson) / *My Kind Of*
                    Love (Jerry Reed)
      Great World Sounds – 1970.
      GWS Records. Recorded in Nashville.

Please note Peter Wynne wrote some of these songs sometimes under the name of Wynne, Williams or Smith.

Sheet music to Peters' 4th single for Parlophone 'The Wall'

THE ZODIACS
1958 - 1965

'The Zodiacs', like almost every band in this era evolved out of a skiffle group. The original members were Keith Hubbard, Butch Bowen and Melvin Ward, Cliff's brother, all from Stourport. This didn't last too long and they soon split up. Later on, in 1959, Butch and Keith got together again, Butch on drums, Keith on guitar and vocals and Mick Birch on bass. Roger Jackson was drafted in on piano, Keith Hubbard's mother giving Roger the piano that she kept in her front room. Later on Nick Miller joined on rhythm guitar and vocals. Three months later Roger Jackson left during a gig at the Sugar Beet Club. They carried on until the spring of 1961 when Nick Miller left to join the Roger Lavern Combo. This was the end of 'The Zodiacs' (MK 1).

A young band called 'The Sceptres' had played support to 'The Zodiacs' at Frank Freemans in May 1961. Keith thought they had potential to help reform 'The Zodiacs'. So he interviewed them at Mick Waldron's parents' house, a fine old listed building, which was situated where Ferndale Estate is now. The interview went well: Colin Youngjohns, Mick Waldron and Roy Campbell joined 'The Zodiacs'.(Things did not fare so well for the old house however. It got severely damaged by fire and had to be demolished).

Early in 1962 'The Zodiacs' began a residency at 'The Fountain' on Friday, Saturday and Sunday nights.

On seeing a couple of brothers turning up from a notorious Stourport fighting family at 'The Fountain' one night, Keith decided immediately that the brothers would be better employed as bouncers than as paying customers.

This situation worked well for about eight months until a gang from Stourbridge who had fallen out with the brothers turned up one night. All hell broke out and there was further trouble the following weekend. 'The Zodiacs' decided to call it a day at 'The Fountain'.

A good booking for the band at this time was the Atlas Ballroom at Stechford in Birmingham, an old converted cinema with a large stage. Colin Youngjohns decided that such a decent venue required good stage gear and duly purchased a bright purple suit from Chetwins, the tailors at the corner of Navigation Street in Birmingham, the only trouble being that the suit had been made for a chap about 6'2" who had fallen down on his payments. Colin being quite a lot shorter, the suit was duly altered and did good for quite a few years.

THE ZODIACS
at 'The Fountain'
left to right
Roy Campbell
Mick Waldron
Keith Hubbard
Mick Birch
Colin Youngjohns

The Zodiacs gigged extensively throughout the Midlands supporting Roy C (Shotgun Wedding) and Chris Montez at Old Hill Plaza and Jerry Lee Lewis at Handsworth Plaza. They also had regular support spots at Kidderminster and Stourbridge Town Halls for the 'Fred Bannister Organisation'. Colin being renamed Earl Grant by Fred Bannister, the band now being called 'Earl Grant and The Zodiacs'. Amongst others they supported at Kidderminster Town Hall, Gene Vincent, Cilla Black and The Walker Brothers. Keith remembers particularly well the night The Walker Brothers played the Town Hall. The American trio were pissed as newts on whisky. During their second set one of the Walker Brothers standing near the front of the stage leant over too far and fell into a whole gang of girls down the front. All Keith could see was a mop of blonde hair, which he grabbed hold of and hauled him back on stage. "Gee thanks man" was the response.

In early 1964 Ken Chatterton replaced Mick Birch on bass and in the autumn of the same year Mick Waldron and Colin Youngjohns left.

When Ken Chatterton became unavailable due to family illness, a crisis was in the making, as there were bookings to fulfil. Mick Thomas from 'The Raiders' was drafted in on rhythm guitar. He in turn got hold of Ian Hardiman and Ray Harris from 'The Ward Five', bass and vocals respectively. The bookings were fulfilled and 'The Zodiacs' MK 3 took off. Early in 1965 Keith Hubbard retired from lead guitar and became manager, Ian Hardiman moved from bass to lead and Rob Newell (also ex Raiders) took over on bass.

Some time later in 1965, Ray Harris the singer departed without warning. This sounded the death knell of 'The Zodiacs' after seven years on the road. However a new band with a new name was to form out of the ashes of the old.

FOOTNOTE

For a while during the later stages of 'The Zodiacs' they had a keyboard player, Mike Preston, who had a claviolene and electric piano. Mike lived in Greatfield Road at the time.

PEOPLE AND EVENTS IN THE NEWS
1956 - 1962

Featuring some local news items that I found interesting in this period, the emphasis of course on music. Information obtained from old copies of the Kidderminster Shuttle.

1956

Wednesday 22nd February

Joe Loss and his Orchestra appear at Kidderminster – The Baths Ballroom.

Monday 5th March

For six days at the Central Cinema the film 'Blackboard Jungle' was shown starring Glenn Ford. The film featured the soundtrack *'Rock Around The Clock'* by Bill Haley and his Comets.

Sunday 3rd June

Kidderminster born Peter Collins won the Belgian Grand Prix at an average speed of 118.3 mph, beating both Stirling Moss and Juan Fangio. This was Peter Collins' first Grand Prix win.

Monday 11th June

James Dean with Natalie Wood appears in the film 'Rebel without a Cause' at the Central Cinema.

Friday 13th July

The Radcliffe Arms on Birchen Coppice opens, the town's first new inn since 1934. Fred Hunt was the first landlord.

Sunday 30th June

Peter Collins wins the French Grand Prix at an average speed of 122.28mph. This puts him in the lead of the world title race ahead of his Ferrari team mate Juan Fangio.

Sunday 2nd September

In a very sporting gesture, Peter Collins hands over his Ferrari to team mate Juan Fangio whose own car was crippled in the pits at the Monza Grand Prix, virtually ceding the title to Fangio. This made him a huge hero among the Italian racing enthusiasts.

Friday 28th September

The Florence Ballroom states in its advert "NO ROCK 'N' ROLL". A more tolerant view was expressed by Bewdley's new Baptist minister, the Rev. David Hudson, who told the Shuttle "I quite like rock 'n' roll, but not when it goes to the extremes of tearing up seats and dancing in cinemas. That's just hooliganism".

Saturday 27th October

Frank Freeman organises first rock 'n' roll dance contest in Kidderminster.

Monday 29th October

The film 'Rock Around the Clock' arrives at the Central   starring 'Bill Haley and The Comets', creating a sensation. Over 3,000 people saw the film on the first day   alone. Teenagers stamped their feet, clapped, kicked their seats and sang. At 5:30 hundreds of young carpet workers headed for the Central forming queues eight deep in places. Jiving broke out in the aisles, but was kept under control by the manager. After the last performance scores of young people hung around in the streets outside, talking in groups. No trouble was reported, and the film was kept on for a few more days. Coaches came from the Black Country, as the   film had been banned there.

After this the whole town went rock 'n' roll mad for a while. Frank Freeman started regular rock 'n' roll sessions on Thursday nights, even Miss Southall relented and allowed a thirty minute rock 'n' roll spot at The Florence. In December The Playhouse put on 'Dave Shand and his Rockin Rhythm All Stars'; all seats 5 shillings, and on Saturday December the 8th there was a rock 'n' roll evening at the Baths Ballroom with the wonderfully named 'Fred Newey and his Radio and Television Orchestra'. Even Bob and Joan Awford's dance studio finished the year at St. Mary's Hall with a Rock 'n' Roll New Year's Eve party.

Friday 14th December

At twenty four years of age Peter Collins of Kidderminster was voted 'Racing Driver of the Year' by the Guild of Motoring Writers.

Friday 21st December

Kidderminster's new college is opened at Aggborough, the £200,000 building being described as an 'Act of Faith'. It will include the first real Department of Carpet Technology.

1957

1957 was a good year for jazz with Mick Mulligan and George Melly appearing at the Playhouse in February and December and many other jazz bands appearing in town this year.

Monday 11th February

Peter Collins married actress Louise Cordier in Miami, Florida. The couple planned to live in Milan, hometown of Ferrari.

Thursday 14th February

Fats Domino appears in the film 'Shake Rattle and Roll' at the Central.

Monday 14th March

Bill Haley and The Comets appear in the film 'Don't Knock the Rock' at the Futurist cinema. Also appearing are The Platters and Little Richard.

Thursday 23rd April

The Queen and The Duke of Edinburgh visit Kidderminster for a short stay. They were greeted by thousands of townspeople, cheering them all the way.

Sunday 28th April

Peter Collins wins the Naples Grand Prix in a Ferrari.

Monday 27th May

The rock 'n' roll film 'The Girl Can't Help It' appears for six days at the Grand cinema, starring Jayne Mansfield, The Platters, Little

Richard, Fats Domino, Gene Vincent and his Bluecaps, and Eddie Cochran. From August onwards skiffle gets a regular spot at the Florence. 'The Severn Valley Skiffle Kings' played there regularly, also 'The Skivers'. In fact skiffle became so popular that an uproarious outdoor skiffle party took place in local beauty spot Habberley Valley on Saturday night/Sunday morning, September the 1st and 2nd. The teenagers jived to the sounds of a five-piece skiffle band, dressed in gaudy sweaters and tight slacks dancing in the glow of car headlights on the springy valley turf. This seems to paint an idyllic picture. However local residents were not amused and called in the police, saying that they had been kept awake until 2:30 in the morning. The revellers left a trail of beer bottles and cans behind them. One of the residents, Mrs Elsie Brown did however pass the remark "If I had been single and a few years younger, I would have joined them".

The young partygoers thought the whole thing was 'Great. We had our own food and drink; the only problem was the damp night air, which kept on slacking off the strings on the double bass'. Even the local religious fundamentalists joined in bearing a banner between two poles declaring 'the wages of sin are death' and singing Salvation Army hymns.

Friday 27th September
Frank Freeman holds a Rock 'n' Roll Skiffle Ball at the Town Hall. Playing on the night were 'The Severn Valley Skiffle Kings' and 'The Skivers'.

Saturday 23rd November
'The Eric Delaney Band' appeared at the Baths Ballroom, Kidderminster.

1958

Saturday 19th March
Peter Collins wins a gruelling 12 hours International Race in Florida at a record average speed, together with co-driver Phil Hill.

Sunday 20th April
Armed teddy boys who had come by train to Kidderminster, were intercepted by police on Comberton Hill, on their way to Stourport.

Dressed in full teddy boy uniform they were carrying various weapons including an iron bar wrapped in a newspaper, and an old saw.

Saturday 3rd May

Peter Collins wins British Grand Prix at Silverstone in a Ferrari.

Monday 12th May

Elvis Presley appears in the film 'Jailhouse Rock' at the Central.

Monday 2nd June

The film 'Disc Jockey Jamboree' is on at the Central, featuring Charlie Gracie, Jerry Lee Lewis, Fats Domino, also Count Basie with Paul Williams.

Monday 14th July

The film version of the '6–5 Special' appears at the Central with Lonnie Donegan, Dickie Valentine and Petula Clark.

Thursday 7th Aug

The funeral took place of racing driver Peter Collins in the tiny Norman church of St. Mary's at Stone. He was killed the previous Sunday taking part in the German Grand Prix at Nuremberg, when his red Ferrari ran off the track. He was twenty-six years old.

Friday 22nd August

The Savoy Jazz Club opens at The Tontine, Stourport.

Saturday 11th October

'Tommy Burton and the Rave Men' open up the dance season at Kidderminster Baths with their 'Rock-a-Beat' music.

Wednesday 22nd October

The Carlton Jazz Club starts at The Black Horse, Kidderminster.

Monday 17th November

Famous pianist Russ Conway appears at The Playhouse.

Friday 26th December

Opening of the Electric Garden Cinema ballroom in Bewdley.

1960

Monday 9th February – Saturday 14th February
The John Osborne play 'Look Back in Anger' is at The Playhouse, principal actors Joe Goodman and Kathleen Kelly. Teddy boy warfare at Stourport over Easter bank Holiday Monday; rival gangs fought each other amongst holidaymakers, one youth had to dive in the river to avoid pursuers. Even the Teddy Girls joined in, hitting each other with their stiletto heels.

Sunday 1st May
Regular Trad and Mod Jazz sessions start at The Playhouse every Sunday.

Tuesday 10th May
Jazz Club opens at the Cross Keys in Worcester Street.

Friday 4th September
Kidderminster's new cattle market opened. It was completed at a cost of £275,000.

Friday 18th September
The Friday Pop Club starts at the New Meeting Hall in the Bull Ring. 'The Cadillacs' were playing that night. This was the first advert for a live rock 'n' roll group.

Wednesday 21st October
The Farmer's Boy pub opens on Comberton Hill. The previous night The Clarendon, also on Comberton Hill, closed, passing its license on to the Farmer's Boy. The Clarendon, one of Kidderminster's oldest pubs, probably had the longest bar in town, at 35 feet. During the late 19th Century it was popular with patrons of the old music hall before the Playhouse existed. It was a common sight to see fifty or sixty pints of beer lined up along the counter, ready for when the customers came in after the show.

1961

Friday 19th February

Police were concerned at rowdyism at the Baths Ballroom. There had been serious disturbances at the Saturday night dances. In future there was to be no admission after 9.30 pm, to stop drunken youths entering the dance hall.

Sunday 21st February

Cliff Richard appears in the film "Expresso Bongo" at the Central, along with Sylvia Sims and Laurence Harvey.

Tuesday 15th March

There was mass emigration to Australia by 84 Kidderminster people (men, women and their children) to work in Brintons new factory in Geelong.

Friday 25th March

The four hundred year old Queen Elizabeth Grammar School at Hartlebury burnt down. I remember this well as I was a pupil at the time (not responsible). We were all sent to be taught at the Bishop of Worcester's Palace in Hartlebury Castle.

Friday 29th April

The Empire Cinema in the Horsefair was demolished to be replaced by a motor showroom.

Tuesday 27th September

Tubby Hayes appears at the Riverside Jazz Club at the Crown in Stourport. The Cross Keys Jazz Club in Kidderminster was also very active in 1960.

Friday 7th October

"Jive plan may set Town Hall shaking" said Stourport councillors, concerned at plans by local café owner Pat Duffy to stage rock 'n' roll dances at Stourport Town Hall. There were fears that the upstairs was not structurally safe. The dances went ahead anyway on Friday October the 7th, the opening acts being 'The Zodiacs' plus guests 'The

Victors'. The councillor's fears were not without justification, when on a Saturday afternoon in 1973 the whole edifice collapsed into the street without warning; luckily no one was hurt.

Saturday 26th November
Local singing star Peter Wynne appears in a Rock 'n' Trad Spectacular at Worcester Gaumont along with Billy Fury, Joe Brown, Tommy Bruce and Dickie Pride, Nelson Keene and the Valentine Girls. The show was a Jack Good Production.

1962

Friday 10th February
The Cross Keys Jazz Club in Worcester Street closes.

Friday 28th April
'The Claviolene Trio' appear at The Fountain.

Sunday 30th April
'The Crestas' appear at Frank Freemans, the first live rock 'n' roll band to play there.

Friday 2nd June
Local residents object to renewal of the music license at the Electric Garden Cinema, Bewdley. They complained about disturbances from noise, fights and couples 'carrying on' in their gardens. The objection must have been overruled because shortly afterwards 'The Clippers' played a couple of gigs there, one event entitled 'Riverside Rock' on June 17th, followed by 'Regatta Rock' on July 1st.

Thursday 9th November
A new Jazz club to open at Kidderminster Town Hall, run by the London Traditional Jazz Society. Bob Wallis and his Storyville Jazzmen were the first band to appear, others to follow included Alex Welsh and Terry Lightfoot.

Monday 8th December
James Dean appears in the film 'East of Eden' at the Central.

Marilyn Monroe appears in the film 'The Misfits' at The Futurist, alongside Clark Gable and Montgomery Cliff. This was the last film all three stars would make.

Saturday 21st December

'The Roger Lavern Combo' make their farewell appearance at The Fountain.

1963

Was a very active year musically, jazz still going strong at the Town Hall with appearances by Chris Barber, Acker Bilk and Humphrey Lyttleton.

Michael Cox with hit song 'Angela Jones' appears at The Baths Ballroom, also 'The Tommy Burton Combo'.

Local bands still going strong include 'The Cadillacs' and 'The Victors'. 'Cliff Ward and the Cruisers' make an early appearance with 'The Cadillacs' on Saturday June 9th at St. Marys Hall.

Thursday 28th June

Lenny Harrison, rhythm guitarist with the 'Rockin' Casanovas' was killed in a car crash near Tenbury Wells. He was twenty-two years old.

Saturday 25th August

Peter Wynne, Parlophone recording and TV star, presents the Netball League Prize at Hartlebury Parish Hall. Dancing to the 'Jimmy Aldridge Band'.

Tuesday 18th September

Carpet Trades new modern office block opened.

Monday 22nd October

'Emile Ford and the Checkmates' play at The Florence.

Friday 26th October
>The famous 'pulpit' in the town centre, where the policeman directed the traffic is demolished.

Friday 14th December
>The Lion Hotel, an old coaching inn at the top of the High Street, was sold to Woolworths. It was to finally close its doors in the summer of 1963, as it was too old and uneconomical to run.

The year ends with, 'Cliff Ward and The Cruisers' appearing at 'The Fountain' on Sunday December 23rd, Christmas Eve, Boxing Night, and New Yea'rs Eve. A new era is beginning.

Al Boden, photo taken in 1960 shortly after Al left the Danville Saints, to go solo playing country music. The guitar was a Swedish made Levin bought on h.p. for 38 guineas from Jack Woodroffes in Birmingham. Al had to take special care of the Levin, when fights used to break out round the old stove in the Peacock Inn, in the Horsefair, where he used

ACKNOWLEDGEMENTS

Special thanks must go to Nick Charles and Tony Goodwin without whom this first chapter would have been virtually impossible. I would also like to thank Johnny Rogers, Mike Davies, Maxie Miller, John Wainwright, Vic Rose, Anthony Smith, Nigel Turrall, Terry Salters, Bill Sedgley, Ian Hardiman, Colin Youngjohns, Captain Crazy, Keith Hubbard, Peter Wynne, Al Boden.

RECOMMENDED READING

Through a Glass Brightly - Nick Charles
Robson Books   ISBN 1 86105-222-7

The Legendary Joe Meek - John Repsch
Cherry Red Books   ISBN 1 - 901447 - 20 - 0

RIP

Terry Davies - The Cadillacs (Vocalist)

CHAPTER TWO
THE BEAT BOOM
1963 – 1967

When I first met Colin Youngjohns on the top floor of Carpet Trades in the winter of 1965, he was just forming a new group, who were to be called 'The Indigo Set'. They went on to become a successful local band of that era. In the same period Jess Roden was singing with the 'Shakedown Sound', Cliff Ward was going strong with his 'Cruisers/Secrets', Stan Webb had just finished with 'Sounds of Blue' and a tall young man from the Black Country, Robert Plant, had also just finished singing for local blues outfit 'The Crawlin' Kingsnakes'. All this talent was shortly to blossom out on a bigger stage, but at this time the real star of the show was Kidderminster Town Hall which, for three magical years from 1963 to 1966, had hosted all the top acts of the time. Everybody played there except 'The Beatles'! For example, 'The Rolling Stones', 'The Yardbirds', 'The Who', 'The Small Faces', Cilla Black and Tom Jones to name just some.

This all came about back in 1961 when a jazz musician and promoter from London, Fred Bannister, had started setting up jazz venues across the country. He asked the local council if he could put jazz on at Kidderminster Town Hall. The Watch Committee met and were none too sure about the unexpected request. However a young, twenty-nine years old councillor, Charles Talbot, who had been a member of Cambridge University jazz club in his student days, told them that in his experience they would have no trouble at all. So it was given a six month trial. It was a great success and lasted for a couple of years. All the great jazz bands of the day played there such as Acker Bilk, Bob Wallis, Chris Barber, Alex Welsh and Terry Lightfoot. By 1963 however, the jazz boom was drawing to a close, but there was a huge explosion in the popularity of beat groups; so Fred Bannister started promoting them at Kidderminster Town Hall and various other venues around the country. The very first gig was 'Mike Berry and The Innocents' on Thursday August 15th 1963, followed on successive Thursdays by 'Brian Poole and The Tremeloes' and 'The Searchers'. In the jazz period a GPO engineer from Stourport, Norman Dickens, had promoted jazz at the Black Horse and also set up the PA systems at the Town Hall for the big name acts. Impressed by Norman's capabilities and looking for help with the new pop promotions, Fred Bannister offered Norman a job with his organisation. At first Norman combined this with his job at the GPO, but it was hard work combining the two, and his bosses took a rather dim view of it. So Norman left the GPO and became a full time promoter. Shortly after, he moved to London and worked from Fred Bannister's office in Knightsbridge. Not that he was there much, Norman's routine was:- Monday, Bath; Tuesday, Wallington (Surrey); Wednesday, Stourbridge; Thursday, Kidderminster; Friday, Leamington; Saturday, Redhill (Surrey), sometimes Dudley. Quite often there was work on Sunday doing the London clubs. It was a punishing schedule but the pay was good, £30 a week plus expenses; the average wages in Kidderminster then was about £10 a week in 1964.

Back in Kidderminster the shows were doing great business but there was a problem; nowhere for the bands to stay prior to the shows. If they had stayed in the town hotels they would have been besieged by their fans. To help the situation Charles Talbot, who lived in a beautiful mansion, Honeybrook House in Franche on the outskirts of town, put the bands up for the afternoon where they could wash, relax and have a meal. Amongst the acts that took advantage of this kind offer were Cilla Black and Tom Jones. Cilla Black had worked for the same firm, BICC, as Charles' father-in-law, so a few of the family came round to meet Cilla and they had a good chat and a laugh. When Tom Jones came, the daily help, her daughter and a friend wanted to meet him so they all came along. Charles' young children were also there. His younger son Nick who was only four or five at the time, said to Tom "I do like you Tom but I prefer The Beatles!". Tom took it in good part, in fact he had been busy that day visiting Lea Castle Hospital and Worcester Cross Youth Club. Charles Talbot's great, great, great grandfather was actually a member of the original organising committee way back in the 1850s, when the money was raised by public subscription for the Town Hall and Corn Exchange. One can only imagine the reaction of these Victorian gentlemen to the acts that would appear on stage there some 110 years later; Mick Jagger prancing about, Eric Clapton's wailing blues guitar and Tom Jones hip shaking antics would surely have given them apoplexy?

At the end of 1965 Norman Dickens moved back to the Midlands after the Saturday night venue changed from Redhill to Bristol. The travelling became too much, and it was more practical to be based locally. At the end of 1966, the 'Big Beat Sessions' at Kidderminster Town Hall stopped. The business had grown up and the bands were starting to charge a lot more money, which ruled out smaller venues like Kidderminster. So Fred Bannister relocated his Midland venues to Leamington and Malvern Winter Gardens, which had bigger capacities. Norman carried on working with Fred for a while, but eventually struck out on his own joining up with Nigel Mills who was promoting at the Black Horse. With Norman's connections they managed to promote some top class acts and also to pick up on the exciting new bands that were breaking out all over the Midlands.

The Black Horse was an old coaching inn that had a ballroom built at the back and was host for many years to resident dance band 'The Carlton Orchestra'. When the groups finished at the Town Hall, Norman and Nigel promoted at this venue three or four times a week. They also put bands on at the newly opened Stourport Civic Centre; it was difficult to put chart acts

The Mayor, Charles Talbot with a group of teenagers at Honeybrooke House.
Standing l to r: Chas, Rod Gilchrist-DJ, Bill Johnson, Dave Deakin (Hangman), Trevor Oliver, Georgina, Roy Price (Kingsnakes), Stuart Mcroy.
Below l to r: Dave Shuck, Eve Deakin, Maverick (Kingsnakes), Sue Bradwell.

on at the Black Horse as they had become so expensive. One glorious exception to this was Joe Cocker. Norman and Nigel had been offered 'Joe and his Grease Band', but they weren't keen on the idea, the name put them off a bit. They mentioned this to Steve Saunders who used to play records there in the interval. Steve had already seen Joe Cocker at the Bluesology Festival at the Chateau and highly recommended him. The very Thursday night that Joe Cocker was booked for the Black Horse, he appeared on Top of the Pops with his amazing version of the Beatles *"With A Little Help From My Friends"* (The show had been pre-recorded on the Wednesday). Needless to say the show was a sell out, the Black Horse was packed to the hilt, and 'Joe Cocker and the Grease Band' went down a storm.

Other top acts that appeared at The Black were 'Taste' with Rory Gallagher, 'Spooky Tooth' and 'The Peddlers'. Other great favourites were 'Jimmy Cliff and the Shakedown Sound', the 'Alan Bown Set' with Jess Roden on vocals. Robert Plant had also appeared there with Midlands group 'Listen' who had some singles out for CBS. Sadly the Black Horse became a victim of the construction of the ring road and was demolished in 1973. Kidderminster Job Centre now stands on the site. Just one hundred yards down the road at the end of Mill Street was the town's other main venue, Frank Freeman's Dance Club. The story of Frank Freeman is so

Town Hall flyer for March 1964. Note support groups names written in.

Kidderminster BIG BEAT Sessions
TOWN HALL

'IT'S A CRAZY WORLD' WITH

THURS. MAR 5th MARTY WILDE *Shades*

AND THE **WILDCATS**

ENGLAND'S FIRST AMERICAN CHART TOPPERS
THE *Simonalls*

THURS. MAR 12th TORNADOS

PLEASE NOTE FOR ONE WEEK ONLY
WE ARE OPEN ON A

Friday, March 20th.
WITH *Raiders*

THE EAGLES

The Fabulous

THURS. MAR. 26th ROLLING STONES

Our apologies for the rather high price, but these fabulous Artists command fantastic fees **Adm 8/6**

7.30-10.45 p.m. **Adm 4/0** (Except March 26th)

2 GROUPS AT EVERY SESSION ✓

1964

60

amazing I shall be devoting a chapter to it later on.

As for the out-of-town venues, the nearest was the Park Attwood at Trimpley, just a few miles from Kidderminster. Set in its own grounds, the Park Attwood was a country mansion which in the 1960s was run as a rather moribund hotel by its owner Margaret Harbach. In 1963 a young Trimpley resident Peter Phillips persuaded Margaret Harbach to let them have the ballroom for his sister Hilary's twenty-first birthday party. They booked 'Tommy and the Crestas' for the dance. The event was a great success and Peter's friends persuaded him to organise regular dances at the Park Attwood; so dances were run every Thursday night by Peter and a friend, Nigel Rees.

'Tommy and the Crestas' appeared there regularly as did 'Cliff Ward and The Cruisers' who were managed at the time by Roger Rowe, whose land bordered onto the Park Attwood. Initially local promoter Norman Dickens booked the bands at the venue, but eventually Nigel and Peter checked out all the bands personally before they were booked for the Park Attwood. In the intervals, two local girls Lynn and Joy, used to spin the records; DJs in those days were still unheard of. One reason the Park Attwood was so successful was that Nigel and Peter used to lay on a Woodstones' free coach service, for girls only, from the Coventry Café in Kidderminster. There was no return bus, but any girl that hadn't obtained a lift on the night, would be personally driven home by either Nigel or Peter.

The Thursday night sessions proved so successful that Margaret Harbach put on bands herself on Saturday nights. Both these nights drew large crowds and parking became a major problem. A car park attendant Bill Smout was employed to keep some kind of order on the chaos that existed down the long drive and in front of the hotel, and it became quite a game between Bill and the young motorists.

One of the most popular and expensive bands they booked were the 'Idle Race' from Birmingham whose guitarist/vocalist Jeff Lynne, later went on to form 'The Electric Light Orchestra' with Roy Wood. As the promotions at the Park Attwood had been so successful, Nigel and Peter branched out running Tuesday nights at the Chateau which they called the Grotto Club. They also promoted an 'All-Niter' at the Chateau featuring another rock star in the making, Robert Plant and his 'Band of Joy', who got paid £37 for the all-night stint. They also ran Sunday nights at Droitwich Winter Gardens and a brief spell at the George in Bewdley, which was never a success.

Thursday nights at the Park Attwood proved doubly lucrative for Margaret Harbach as they coincided with the top groups appearing at Kidderminster Town Hall, many of whom stayed the night at the hotel. These included 'The Hollies', 'The Swinging Blue Jeans', Dave Dee and his crew, and 'Wayne Fontana and the Mindbenders'. Upon arriving at the Park Attwood, a lot of these musicians would soon be on the dance floor chatting up the local girls. Sometimes when the dance had finished an impromptu jam session would happen until the early hours of the morning; the ballroom echoing to different versions of their latest hits.

In 1965 Nigel and Peter took over the management of 'Cliff Ward and the Cruisers' from their neighbour at Trimpley, Roger Rowe They managed Cliff during the period of his first record *'Candy To Me'*. In 1970 Margaret Harbach sold the Park Attwood to Gordon Allard, owner of the Fountain, who wanted to turn it into an upmarket hotel. The dances stopped after seven years; this highly popular dance venue, featuring all the top local bands, finally came to a halt.

There were two other out-of-town venues that featured prominently on the local beat scene. Although not strictly speaking in our geographical area both were inextricably linked with local groups and their fans. The first of these The Wharf at Holt Fleet was a modest tavern situated right on the banks of the river Severn, not far from Ombersley. Sometime in the 1950s an ambitious landlord had built a small dance hall/function room on the side of the building to help provide entertainment for the caravaners who had permanent sites on the nearby fields. When burly ex-policeman Jim Quinn took over the pub he regularly booked in local bands at the Wharf such as 'The Clippers'.

One disadvantage of the Wharf's pleasant position on the banks of the river Severn meant that every time the river burst its banks it was left in splendid isolation, surrounded by watery fields. Not to be deterred Jim Quinn would transport the group, their gear and the fans on his flat bed truck.

When the beat boom really took off Jim Quinn, encouraged by his daughters and helped by the ubiquitous Norman Dickens who had the contacts, began booking top groups for his Startime Show on Sunday nights.   For a while, acts like 'The Nashville Teens', 'Joe Cocker', 'Skip Bifferty' and 'Chris Farlow' could be seen there. On one occasion Brian Auger appeared with Julie Driscoll on vocals, when their single *'This Wheels on Fire'* was in the top ten. I was there myself that night and will never forget the look of sheer amazement on Julie Driscoll's face as she went through their set, playing on a postage stamp stage in a small function room, in a pub, in a field that to her must have felt like the middle of nowhere.

The other out of town venue situated just a few miles west of The Wharf was the Chateau Impney. The Chateau sits in its own grounds on the outskirts of Droitwich, and is as far removed from the Wharf as a building could possibly be. Built between 1869 and 1875 by local salt magnate John Corbett as a present to his wife, a beautiful French governess he had fallen in love with during a visit to Paris, he built it in the style of a French Chateau. It was, and still is, an impressive building.

After being taken over by the military during the second world war it was pretty run down when it was bought by pub entrepreneur Ralph Edwards, who owned a chain of twenty seven pubs. Ralph Edwards spent a lot of money on it putting on dinner dances, cabaret etc, and dimming the lights for a night club atmosphere. He also had a conservatory built with heating for orange trees and the grounds were landscaped with sunken gardens. But by the early 1960s it needed more investment and Ralph Edwards leased it out to local businessman Eric Pillon. Because of an anomaly in the local licensing laws, it was possible to have a casino and late licensing hours throughout the week and dances were also allowed on Sundays. Eric Pillon took full advantage of these loopholes and some businessmen from Birmingham ran a casino on the first floor. His young son Graham, who was only fifteen at the time, set about fitting a state-of-the-art sound system in the cellar bar, known as the Imp Bar. He imported thirty eight speakers from America. Some were fitted flush into the walls, while others were installed in old unused chimney breasts, which became massive sound chambers. In 1966 the Cellar Bar began being used for live groups. Tuesday nights were known as the Grotto Club, run by Peter Phillips and Nigel Rees from the Park Attwood. But the most exciting innovation came with the start of the Friday night 'All-Niters' promoted by two Kidderminster entrepreneurs, Paul Turner, former bass player with 'Shades 5' and partner in trendy men's boutique Mr Casual at the end of Worcester Street, and John Carter former 'Shades 5' manager who also ran a hairdressing salon in Marlborough Street. They had been inspired by the 'All- Niters' they had seen at the Twisted Wheel Club in Manchester. There was a growing mod scene in Kidderminster and they had searched high and low to find a suitable local venue without any luck when Graham Pillon suggested they try the Cellar Bar at the Chateau. The rental for the night was £100, a lot of money in those days, but Paul and John reckoned they could make a profit, and started searching venues like the Elbow Room looking for new talent for their all-nighters.

One of the first bands they booked were the 'Delroys', one of the new wave of black soul bands coming out of Birmingham. Another great act was Ronnie Jones, an American ex-service man who was fronting his own band in the UK. They also booked 'Herbie Goins and the Nightimers', 'The Idle Race', 'Band of Joy' and 'The Maze' (who included Ian Pearce and Rod Evans, later to join 'Deep Purple'). It was at this time that regular DJs were starting to be used; 'Nick and Fizz' from Kidderminster were the main DJs at the all-nighters and built up a solid reputation for being bang up to date with the latest and hippest sounds. Essential to the all-nighter's success was good publicity. This was done by fly posting, not so easy in those days as there were far more police patrolling the streets than there are now; they had to be stuck up very quickly. They had some superb posters that were designed by Pete Waldron (ex 'Shakedown' bassist) and Mike Hardiman.

John Carter and Paul Turner were not the only promoters. Eric Pillon had contacts and the agencies soon got to know the place, and many now legendary rhythm'n'blues acts from London came up to the Chateau to perform. Graham Bond was one I particularly remember, who played his Hammond Organ nearly all night with just a drummer for accompaniment, slept over, and then played again the following afternoon. Totally captivating music and a great memory. Someone else I remember seeing there was 'Long John Baldry,' who, while eating his dinner in the upstairs room on a boiling hot summer's evening, decided he wanted to enjoy the view and the evening sunshine, so he asked the waiter to move the table outside onto the balcony where he finished his meal 'al fresco'. Mulling over his wine he is reported to have written the lyrics to his only hit *Let The Heartaches Begin'*.

Graham Pillon ran his own club on Sunday nights through 1967/68, called The Lady Jane Club. It had a laid back feel with more sophisticated sounds, a little French music, modern jazz and the occasional pianist , when they hauled the grand piano down from upstairs. In 1968 the Chateau put on an open air festival calling it Bluesology. With John Peel as DJ, bands appearing included 'The Move', 'Fleetwood Mac,' 'Joe Cocker' and 'Geno Washington'. I visited the festival on a trip home from London and saw Joe Cocker for the first time, he made quite an impact. Unfortunately the festival was plagued by downpours of rain on and off all day.

Towards the end of the 1960s the police were getting fed up with the free and easy ways of the Chateau due to the liberal licensing laws and rumours of drug dealing, so the Chateau was raided. No arrests were made and the venue was not closed down. However Eric Pillon got fed up with the situation and put in a management team to run it for a while. He eventually got a loan to buy the property outright but didn't keep it long and the Chateau was sold in 1971. Graham Pillon carried on his interest in sound and lighting with the very successful Electric Stage Company, installing sound and lighting equipment in night clubs, concerts, conferences, fashion shows, raves etc.

I was a regular visitor to the Chateau, during that summer of love of 1967. The magic began when you drove through the parklands over the small bridge, pulling up on the gravel drive, you were welcomed by Mac, a Macaw Parrot, who didn't suffer drunks gladly if they decided to play with him. Mac the Macaw once eat a hotel guest's brogues when they were left out to be polished, turning them into a pair of sandals overnight. When the Chateau changed hands in 1971, Peter Bratt offered Mac a home for a bit, but he was impossible to look after and ended his days in the West Midlands Safari Park.

Turning to the left you walked down the stairs to the Imp Bar which stayed open until 2am, a great advantage in the days of 10.30 closing. Bacardi and Coke was the 'in' drink of the day, usually served up by Deiter or Konrad, the two German barmen employed by the Chateau.

*Kidderminster Mods
Summer 1965*

*Front Row: l to r
Sean Jenkins, Jess
Roden(Shakedowns),
Mick Snell.
Middle Row: Nick
Clegg(Dj. Nick n' Fizz),
Ian Watts (Crawlin
Kingsnakes), Les Deakin
Top: Ken Swannell
Photo : Ken Swannell*

If you had brought a girl or met a girl there, the night often ended up with passionate embraces in the car; the setting of John Corbett's beautiful chateau, built for his young French bride, being the perfect location for making love.

In spite of the erotic charms of the Chateau, the burgeoning progressive rock scene at Frank Freeman's and my first attempts at promoting in the back room of the Old Pheasant in Worcester, I had made up my mind to move to London in the spring of 1968 together with Martin Harrison drummer with 'The Indigo Set'. Martin wanted to further his drumming career and I had vague aspirations of becoming a road manager and living a life of fun and freedom. So for the second time in my life I was leaving home, not this time to the south west and the open seas, but to the south east, to London, and what ever lay beyond.

THE CHATEAU IMPNEY, DROITWICH.

*Built in 1875.   It had 3,000 men working
on it at one time. The architect was
Auguste Tronquoise*

TOWN HALL DATES
OCTOBER 1963 – DECEMBER 1966

Unfortunately I have been unable to list every Town Hall gig with the correct date so rather than give wrong information, I have listed every group or act that appeared at the Town Hall. I have given the dates of some of the more famous groups, where I believe they are correct. It must be remembered that many big name bands like 'The Who' and 'The Moody Blues' played the Town Hall on a number of occasions. I would particularly like to thank Dave Bodley and Paul Jennings for their help. The first documented Big Beat Session was by 'Mike Berry and The Innocents' on Thursday August 15th 1963 and the last by 'Herbie Goins and the Nightimers', on Thursday December 1st 1966.

THE GROUPS
OCTOBER 1963 – DECEMBER 1966

THE ACTION
THE ANIMALS (2)
THE APPLEJACKS (2)
THE ARTWOODS
THE BATMAN AND ROBIN SHOW
CLIFF BENNETT AND THE REBEL ROUSERS
DAVE BERRY AND THE CRUISERS (3)
MIKE BERRY AND THE INNOCENTS (15-08-1963)
THE BIG THREE (2)
CILLA BLACK (02-04-1964)
THE BROOKS BROTHERS
JOE BROWN AND HIS BRUVVERS
TOMMY BRUCE AND THE BRUISERS
CATCH THE MEASLES
NEIL CHRISTIAN AND THE CRUSADERS
CRISPIAN ST. PETERS
THE CRYING SHAMES
DAVE DEE, DOZY, BEAKY, MICK AND TICH
THE SPENCER DAVIS GROUP (2)
DONOVAN (19-08-1965)
THE DOWNLINERS SECT (2)
THE EAGLES (FROM BRISTOL) (2)
BERN ELLIOT AND THE FENMEN
SHANE FENTON AND THE FENTONES

WAYNE FONTANA AND THE MINDBENDERS
THE FORTUNES
THE FOURMOST
    THE FOUR PENNYS
        FREDDY AND THE DREAMERS (27.04.1964)
        HERBIE GOINS AND THE NIGHTIMERS (01.12.1966)
        GOLDIE AND THE GINGERBREADS
        HEDGEHOPPERS ANONYMOUS
        HEINZ AND THE WILD ONES
        HERMANS HERMITS
        THE HOLLIES (3)
        THE IN CROWD
        THE INTERNS
        TONY JACKSON AND THE VIBRATIONS
        TOM JONES (22.04.1965)
        JOHNNY KIDD AND THE PIRATES
        THE KINKS (2)
        JOHN LEYTON
        THE LONG AND THE SHORT
        ST. LOUIS UNION (2)
        MANFRED MANN (3)
THE MERSEYBEATS (3)
THE MERSEYS
THE MINDBENDERS (2)
THE MOJOS (2)
THE MOODY BLUES (3)
THE NATURALS
THE NASHVILLE TEENS
PINKERTONS   ASSORTED
COLOURS
THE POETS
BRIAN POOLE AND THE
TREMELOES (3)
THE PRETTY THINGS (2)
TOMMY QUICKLY AND
THE REMO FOUR
THE REDCAPS
THE RIOT SQUAD
THE ROCKIN BERRIES (3)
THE ROLLING STONES (26.03.1964)
PAUL AND BARRY RYAN
RUSS SAINTY AND THE NU-NOTES
SCREAMING LORD SUTCH AND THE SAVAGES)
THE SEARCHERS (3)
THE SMALL FACES (2)
THE SONS OF FRED
SOUNDS INCORPORATED (2)
THE SPOTNICKS
THE SWINGING BLUE JEANS (3)

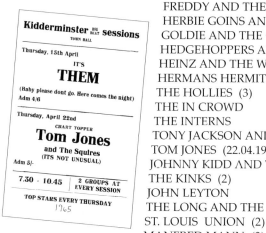

THEM (15.04.1965)
THE TORNADOS
THE TROGGS
TWINKLE
THE UGLYS
THE UNDERTAKERS
GENE VINCENT AND THE SHOUTS
UNIT 4 + 2 (2)
THE WALKER BROTHERS (08.07.1965)
THE WHO (3)
MARTY WILDE
THE YARDBIRDS (3)
THE ZOMBIES (4)

FOOTNOTE

Mention here must be made of Brian Wilson who, together with Martin Stook and later Nigel Mills, promoted in the area under the name of Startime Promotions between 1961 and 1966. Using mainly local groups like 'Tommy and the Crestas' and 'Cliff Ward and the Cruisers', their main venues were the Mare and Colt and Cleobury Village Hall (both on Friday) the Chateau on Sundays, and Saturday nights at Kidderminster Town Hall. Brian started work at Long's Radio Shop in Mill Street when he left School, and went on to sell records from there. He supplied Blue Beat and Ska Records via London wholesalers to sell to the mods and later went on to supply more obscure West Coast Records via One Stop and Musicland to Frank Freeman's. He also supplied the records to the Black Horse. When Long's was demolished he opened his own record shop, Sounds Around, in the Swan Centre, which was successful for many years until it closed down in 1993 due to a huge increase in rent. Martin Stook has carried on as a mobile DJ, operating under the name of 'The Oldest DJ in Town'. Nigel Mills formed an agency with Norman Dickens called NORSAN and promoted with Norman at the Black Horse and Stourport Civic Centre. Nigel sadly died in March 2000.

Bags from local record stores
preserved by Andy Silvester

THE GROUPS

1963 – 1967

THE ACCELERATORS-THE HUSKIES-THE PROFITS
THE BOGEYMEN
CENSORED
THE COUNTERPOINTS-THE APPER CLARSE
CUSTARD TREE
BIG DAVE AND THE HANGMEN
FRANKENSTEINS BLUE DEVILS - ORBIT FIVE
THE INDIGO SET
THE JAVELINS - THE CRAWLING KINGSNAKES
MONEY JUNGLE
NORMAN'S CONQUESTS
THE RAIDERS
THE SCORPIONS
THE SIMONALS
STRANGERS INCORPORATED - SHADES FIVE
SOUNDS OF BLUE - **CHICKEN SHACK**
THE STRINGBEATS
THE SUNSETTERS - THE SHAKEDOWN SOUND
JIMMY CLIFF AND THE SHAKEDOWN SOUND
THE BAND OF JOY
TOMMY AND THE CRESTAS
CLIFF WARD AND THE CRUISERS - MARTIN
RAYNOR AND THE SECRETS
THE WARD FIVE
THE WHIRLWINDS

Other groups active in the area from the early days included 'The Victors', 'The Invaders' and 'The Zodiacs'. 'The Clippers' rocked throughout the beat boom period and didn't finally split up until 1967. 'Eddy and the Kings' also played during this time.

THE ACCELERATORS
1962 - 1964

'The Accelerators' were formed in 1962 by Butch Humber – vocals, Robbie Blunt, guitar and Micky Benson, drums. They were all school friends from Wolverley and used to rehearse at Robbie Blunt's parents' house in Sebright Road. They played all the local youth clubs and also the Bridge Inn in Kidderminster, they were later joined by Gough Taylor on bass and Alan Hutton on rhythm. Their best gig was playing outside the Queen's Head in Wolverley at the annual Wolverley carnival, where a stage had been set up. The star guest that year was June Morton of 'Tinga and Tucka' fame. The band split up in 1964 when they all left school. Butch Humber went on to join...

THE HUSKIES
1964 – 1966

With Butch on vocals the line up was Richie McGowan, lead; Dave Conway, rhythm; and Mick Dickenson, bass. They originally had a guy called Dave on drums, but he was soon replaced by Bill Simmons. 'The Huskies' soon became very popular.

They were all very young, Bill Simmons was only fourteen. They were in effect the boy band of that era compared to grown up acts like 'Tommy and the Crestas' and 'Cliff Ward and the Cruisers'. 'The Huskies' had some great support spots at both Kidderminster and Stourbridge Town Halls including 'The Troggs' at Stourbridge telling them they'd have a great night at Kidderminster the next day. Unfortunately this didn't happen. The Kidderminster fans didn't take kindly to the Troggs and booed them throughout their set.

When Donovan came to the Town Hall his band hadn't turned up, so 'The Huskies' were called in an emergency to help with the show. They were actually setting their gear up while Donovan did his solo act. Although popular with the girls at the front, some of the lads at the back got a bit restless, shouts of 'Dylan', and a few chairs, brought Donovan's act to a swift close. When the Kidderminster Shuttle reporter went to interview Donovan, he had to do it with Donovan locked inside the dressing-room toilet.

THE HUSKIES
 at the Black Horse,
March 1966.
l to r: Mick Dickenson,
Butch Humber,
Bill Simmonds,
Dave Conway,
Richie Mcgowan

Another person with unhappy memories of Kidderminster must have been Barry Jenkins, drummer with the 'Nashville Teens' who, while loading the van, was threatened by a bunch of yobs who started banging on the sides of the van. The drummer brandished a shotgun at them which only incensed the mob even more, so he quickly had to reverse the van to the rear of the yard, while somebody shut the iron gates. He eventually managed to get out by hiding in the back seat of Fred McGowan's car. Fred, father of the Huskies guitarist Richie, dropped the drummer off in Worcester Road where he rejoined the rest of 'The Nashville Teens'. He later had to return to Kidderminster to face charges.

'The Huskies' also supported 'The Who' at Kidderminster Town Hall. Amazed at 'The Whos' stage equipment and Keith Moon's drum kit, they were even more knocked out to be told by the group's roadies that they could use their gear. This actually really didn't do them any favours; everybody got carried away competing with each other and the balance went out of the window. Another great gig for 'The Huskies' was supporting 'The Small Faces' at Malvern Winter Gardens. Butch knocked on their dressing room door and asked Steve Marriott if he minded 'The Huskies' doing *What You Gonna Do About It*' as it was part of their set. "No problem mate, you do it" said Steve. When they played the number, they heard another set of drums playing behind them, peeping behind the stage curtains they saw Steve Marriott playing the drums, total concentration written all over his face.

In November 1966 Richie McGowan and Dave Conway left the band. They were replaced by ex 'Simonal' Ian Simmons on guitar and Bob Baker, a keyboard player from Hereford. This led to a change of name and they now became 'The Profits' (1966 – 1967).

In March 1967, Mick Dickenson the bass player left and was replaced by Tony Godfrey. This only lasted a few months when Butch and Tony Godfrey had a major bust-up at the Labour Club, which led to actual fisticuffs, the upshot being Tony Godfrey left and was replaced by Colin Hepwood (ex 'Raiders'). 'The Profits' carried on for a couple of months, but the impetus had gone and they split up in May 1967.

Butch then spent a short period with 'The Reflections'; ten gigs in all. In September 1967 Butch, together with drummer Bill Simmons, Rob Newell, bassist with the 'Indigo Set', and Bill Davies, ex 'Shakedowns' on guitar, played a one-off gig, calling themselves 'River Styx Crossing' as a memorial to Fred McGowan, 'The Huskies' ex-manager who had recently died,   to raise money for his widow. Butch later went on to team up with Bill Davies to join r 'n' b group 'Money Jungle'.

THE BOGEYMEN

1963 – 1967

'The Bogeymen' were formed towards the end of 1962 when brothers Pete and Harry Bishop approached ex-'Skiffle King' Tony Goodwin with the idea of forming a group. Tony was keen as his last band 'The Casanovas' had split up a month before. Richard Yates was drafted in on bass, the only trouble being that he didn't have a guitar. This was no problem to the ever resourceful Tony Goodwin, who duly made him one based on a Vox Phantom.

So rehearsals began in the Bishop brother's home, The Anchor in Welch Gate, Bewdley. Although the pub had been closed for three years they still lived there and the pub had an upstairs function room which was perfect for rehearsals. 'The Bogeymen' started their career at the Little Lakes Country Club just outside Bewdley; their manager at this time was Bill Cordle, Tony's partner in the 'Casanovas'. Bill, a lovely chap, was no great shakes as a manager; he generally booked himself into venues as a solo act rather than getting the group work. So they took on Colin Pierce as manager who had the great advantage of a car to take them to gigs. A year later they acquired a road manager in the form of Bill Ince, a local undertaker, who carried the gear in one of his firms funeral hearses. The band paid him £1 a gig, whether it be Wribbenhall Parish Hall or some club the other side of Walsall.

After the usual round of village halls and pubs and clubs, the group started getting some better gigs, including support spots at Stourbridge Town Hall to 'The MerseyBeats' and 'Dave Dee, Dozy, Beaky, Mick and Titch'. They even managed to headline one night at Kidderminster Town Hall. They were in the audience when they were asked if they could do the headline spot as main band, 'UK Bonds' couldn't make the gig. Although Tony said he was not psychologically prepared, they were dragged on stage anyway. Tony was delighted that he could use the support band's Vox amplifiers ('The Huskies') instead of the Selmer amps that they normally used.

In September 1965 they supported 'The Fortunes' at the Silver Glades Ice Rink in Birmingham, at the height of 'The Fortunes' popularity with their single '*You've Got Your Troubles*' riding high in the charts. The support band had to play on a narrow platform only 4 feet wide suspended some eight

THE BOGEYMEN
*at The Anchor in Bewdley.
left to right: Colin Pierce, Bill Ince, Ken Beeston, Richard Yates, Pete Bishop Tony Goodwin, Harry Bishop*

feet above the main stage. The band had to stand in a line to play. At that height the heat was terrific coming off the dance floor, so after their set Tony hung his sweat soaked shirt over the drum kit. As the curtains opened for 'The Fortunes' set, there was Tony's shirt suspended proudly above their lead singer's head.

In the Christmas of the same year they supported 'The Pretty Things' at Malvern Winter Gardens. When 'The Pretty Things' didn't turn up, 'The Bogeymen' had to fill the gap; their hour's worth of material had to be stretched out pretty thin. When 'The Pretty Things' eventually turned up they borrowed 'The Bogeymen's' gear, wild man drummer Viv Prince broke all the drum sticks, while bass player John Stax blew up their bass amp. Such are the trials and tribulations of support acts.

In 1966 they won a beat contest at Tenbury Wells Carnival, the prize being a support spot that evening at the Swan Hotel in Tenbury to ('*Got To Get You Into My Life*') 'Cliff Bennett and Rebel Rousers'. 1967 was a bad year for 'The Bogeymen', their manager Colin Pierce died of cancer; he was only 24 years old. On the day Colin died, Richard Yates was involved in a serious car accident and was hospitalised for some time. He eventually recovered and they played a few more gigs, the last one being at Frank Freeman's, where drummer Pete Bishop got into trouble with Mrs. Freeman for hammering a wooden block deep into the dance floor to stop his kit from moving forward. Shortly after Richard Yates got married and moved to Hong Kong. The band split up, family commitments and changes in musical taste brought the career of 'The Bogeymen' to a close.

CENSORED

1967 – 1968

At the end of 1966, Dave Bodley (ex 'Orbit 5'), Dave Tiplady (ex 'Invaders') and Colin Hepwood (ex 'Raiders') joined up with 'Norman's Conquests' (Norman Clarke, vocals) for rehearsals at the Half Moon. Dave Tiplady soon took over from Norman Clarke on vocals and Dave Holder the bass player joined the new line up, which was; Dave Tiplady, vocals; Colin Hepwood, guitar; Dave Holder, bass; Dave Bodley, drums. The group called themselves 'Censored'.

The Gun Tavern in Worcester was one of their regular gigs, and while playing there, their manager Barry Finch introduced them to keyboard player Grant Balmer, who soon joined the band. Apart from regular appearances at The Gun Tavern they also played The Wharf, and had a support spot to Cardiff band 'Electric Underground' at the Malvern Winter Gardens. Colin Hepwood left the band at the end of November when Ian Simmonds (ex 'Simonals') joined the group on guitar. The band split up in January 1968. A month later Dave Bodley joined Robbie Blunt and Johnny Pasternak to form rock trio 'Liquorice'.

THE COUNTERPOINTS
1963 – 1965

'The Counterpoints' were school friends at King Charles High School. Dave Towers, Alan Reynolds and Al Jacobs all had a mutual interest in the instrumental groups of the day like 'The Ventures' and 'The Shadows'. During the summer of 1963 they were joined by Bob Wanklyn on drums and Bobby Allison on vocals. Their first gig was at the Half Moon on a Sunday night in November 1963. Bobby Allison had stage fright and didn't sing a note, so they had to do a totally instrumental set which fortunately for them they had rehearsed well. Bobby Allison was soon replaced by another school friend Roger Cohen and further gigs followed at the Half

Moon, Shenstone Training College and the Fountain (supporting 'Earl Grant and the Zodiacs').

The line up at this time was Roger Cohen – vocals, Al Reynolds and Al Jacobs – guitars, Dave Towers – bass and Bob Wanklyn – drums. The name 'Counterpoints' was taken from a number by 'The Ventures' based on counterpoint harmonies. Shortly after they bought a couple of AC30 amps from 'The Raiders', who had just split up.

THE COUNTERPOINTS WITH DAVE BERRY at Stourbridge Town Hall March 1965.
l to r Roger Steward, Dave Towers, Roger Cohen, Al Jacobs, Al Reynolds.
Sitting: Dave Berry
Photo: Dave Towers

On the 25th June 1964 they had their first support spot at Kidderminster Town Hall, supporting 'Tommy Quickly and the Remo Four'. Dave Towers remembers the tension in the band before this gig, the Town Hall being the equivalent of them playing at Wembley at that time. Their second booking at the Town Hall was supporting 'The Mojos' on July 23rd 1964. By this time they had acquired a manager in Ken Morris who replaced Bob Wanklyn on the drums with Roger Steward. Their third major support spot was at Stourbridge Town Hall supporting 'The Animals' when *House Of The Rising Sun*' was number one in the charts. As 'The Counterpoints' struck up their first number, John Lee Hookers *'Dimples'*, the curtains opened and a wave of heat hit the band from the audience of 1,200 packed into the hall like sardines; Dave Towers shirt was soaked through in thirty seconds. Further support spots followed with 'The Undertakers', 'The Koobas', 'Dave Berry', 'Unit 4 + 2' and 'Johnny Kidd and the Pirates'.

During the spring and summer of 1965 Dave Towers played five gigs with 'The Dischords'.

Colin Youngjohns was singing temporarily for them. In the autumn of 1965 he left 'The Dischords', it was at this point that 'The Counterpoints' and 'The Hangmen' merged to form........

THE APPER CLARSE
1965 – 1967

The line up was Roger Cohen – vocals, Larry Harris, lead guitar; Dave Jones, bass; Ken Lewis, rhythm and Roger Steward, drums. The name was thought up by Larry Harris. (Larry and Ken Lewis were at that time writing scripts for Irish comedian Dave Allen). Their uniform was made up by local gentleman's tailor Hodge and Hand in Oxford Street. It was a sixties pastiche of 'toffs' clothing, bright yellow shirts over black T-shirts, with tightly checked flared trousers. The usual round of gigs followed including another support spot to 'The Koobas' at Malvern Winter Gardens and a rather down at heel 'Them' minus Van Morrison at Tamworth. 'Them' turned up without any equipment and had to borrow 'The Apper Clarse's. They were also getting work from the Mercian Agency and a German tour was arranged for November. At this point Dave Towers left, not being entirely happy with the situation. A bass player from Stourbridge was drafted in but didn't stay long and the 'Apper Clarse' went to Germany as a four piece with Ken Lewis moving over to bass. They thoroughly enjoyed their time there, but in spite offers of work in Denmark and Germany, they decided to return home in February 1967. The German trip had turned out to be a bit of a financial disaster, they had to sell all their gear to clear their debts, this was the end of the 'Apper Clarse'.

CUSTARD TREE
1967 – 1968

'Custard Tree', originally a trio, were formed early in 1967 when Jim Boden approached George Kristic with the idea of forming a band; Jim's cousin Dave Smith had a double drum kit and with Jim on guitar and George on bass they all shared vocals. George had chosen to play bass guitar as he had been influenced by Maverick, bass player with 'The Crawling Kingsnakes' when they used to rehearse at the family home, Winbrook House in Welch Gate, Bewdley. George's parents came from Yugoslavia and encouraged him to play the accordion while a pupil at Bewdley High School. He eventually sold the accordion to buy a guitar, much to his mother's disappointment.

After a short period of rehearsals they started getting gigs, originally playing blues and soul numbers and later on progressive rock. They soon impressed local agent Norman Dickens who was running the Norsan Agency at the time, and regular gigs followed at venues such as Droitwich Winter Gardens, Cheltenham Town Hall and Builth Wells. In August 1967 they had a prestigious support spot to 'John Mayall's Bluesbreakers' at Malvern Winter Gardens. They were later joined by Mike Casey on keyboards and Roy Robbins on vocals. While supporting American girl vocal group 'Reparata and the Delrons' at Droitwich Winter Gardens ('*Captain of Your Ship*'– hit single), Mike Casey sat in with them on the keyboards. Another regular gig for the band was the famous Cedar Club in Birmingham. In August 1968 Mike Casey left and was replaced by Abdul Benson. Abdul had been an original member of George's school band at Bewdley High School. The band split up in October 1968 due to the usual musical differences. George and Abdul Benson went on to form 'Wise Virgin'.

BIG DAVE AND THE HANGMEN
1963 – 1965

Sometime in December 1962 Pete Longmore was sitting in a bus going down town when he bumped into Larry Harris and was bemoaning the fact that he had lost his friend and singer from Franche, Jess Roden to 'The Raiders'. Jess often used to sing into a reel-to-reel tape recorder at Pete's home while Pete would beat out time to songs like Tommy Roe's *'Sheila'*.

Larry said he had a friend at St. Ambrose's, Dave Deakin, a would-be singer who was looking to join a band. So together with Ken Lewis and Bill Davies, 'Big Dave and the Hangmen' was formed, Dave Deakin being all of five foot nothing tall.

BIG DAVE AND THE
HANGMEN
at St. Ambroses. l to r
Brian Davies, Larry
Harris, Pete Longmore,
Dave Deakin, Ken Lewis

Rehearsals began at the Deakin's home in Chester Road North and also at St. Ambrose's Youth Club. The line up was Dave Deakin, vocals; Larry Harris, lead guitar; Brian Davies, bass; Ken Lewis, rhythm and Pete Longmore, drums. (School friend Oresti Howard had been an original member but left very early on). They had a hangman's noose for a stage prop which had flashing lights on it. To complete the macabre image Dave Deakin wore a long black wig and a cape and came on stage wielding a club, while the band launched into *'Jack The Ripper'*. Another favourite number was '*Monster Mash*' by 'Boris Pickett and the Crypt Kickers'.

One of their first gigs was at the Black Horse where they played in the interval between the 'Carlton Orchestra Dance Band'. They were a bit worried about how they'd go down, but as soon as they struck up, the audience went wild, dancing and clapping and shouting for encores. In July 1963 'The Hangmen' won a talent contest at St. John's Parish Hall. From then on they played virtually every village hall and youth club in the area and they eventually got support spots at Kidderminster and Stourbridge Town Halls to 'The Applejacks', 'The Honeycombs' and 'The Walker Brothers'.

In the spring of 1965 Brian Davies left and was replaced on bass by Dave Towers from 'The Counterpoints'. Shortly afterwards Dave Deakin left. This was the end of 'Big Dave and the Hangmen'. The rest of the band got in ex-'Zodiacs' Colin Youngjohns on vocals. This band didn't last long, known as 'The Discords' they played the Park Attwood, The Chateau and Oaklands Club during the summer of 1965, before Colin Youngjohns left to eventually join 'The Indigo Set'. The others stayed together, got in 'The Counterpoints' vocalist and drummer to form **'The Apper Clarse'** .

FRANKENSTEIN'S BLUE DEVILS
1963 - 1964

'The Blue Devils' were formed by two Wolverley brothers Elmer and Danny O'Shea, lead and bass respectively, with next door neighbour Mick Kohler on drums, all pupils at Sion Hill. Amongst other venues, they played the Labour Club, the Fountain (in the interval to a dance band), and Kidderminster Cricket Club, where they played in a large marquee along with 'The Simonals' and 'Big Dave and the Hangmen'. Their material was mostly rock 'n' roll classics plus 'The Rolling Stones' '*Its all over Now*' and a few 'Beatles' numbers. 'The Blue Devils' finished towards the end of 1964. Mick Kohler had drifted away and a new group was formed, who went under, the name of.....

ORBIT FIVE
1964 - 1966

The line up was Elmer O'Shea, lead guitar; Danny O'Shea, bass; Mick Betson, drums, and keyboard player Bob Baker. Bob was from Hereford and had played with 'Lee Star and The Astrals' and while working in Kidderminster he met the others in Worcester Cross Youth Club where they were rehearsing. 'Orbit Five' were quite commercial and got plenty of work in the Black Country. They also played Wolverley Memorial Hall, the Nautical William and Old Hill Plaza, where they supported 'Carl Wayne and the Vikings', who Elmer freely admits blew 'Orbit Five' right off the stage. 'The Vikings' were a very impressive outfit who later went on to become 'The Move'.

Towards the end of 1965 there were personnel changes in 'Orbit Five'. Dave Bodley came in on drums and an extra guitarist, Jim Boden was added. This line up was more influenced by the blues, doing numbers by people like Freddy and BB King. However not everybody was into the blues, Elmer recalls playing a gig at Stourport Youth Club one night when the youth leader came up to them halfway through their set and told them "You are the worst band I've ever heard!" So they had to pack up and go home. Shortly after this Jim Boden left, Danny moved over to rhythm guitar and Colin Hepwood came in on bass. Tragically Danny O'Shea died of cancer in July 1966, the band split up and Elmer stopped playing for quite a while.

THE INDIGO SET

1966-1968

In 1964 Colin Youngjohns was working as a colourist at Brintons in the Yarn House where it was warm and comfortable, a great place to have a kip after a hard night's gigging; he was with the Zodiacs at the time. Together with the other lads there he used to climb on top of the stacks of yarn skeins where they built their own dens and played cards. Colins sleep was often rudely interrupted by the foreman shouting 'Elvis' when he was looking for him; in the end the management became tired of this and he got the sack. He then worked at Carpet Trades in the stock records department where I first met him. While at Brintons one of Colin's workmates was a girl called Jane Hatton who was going out with a drummer from Birmingham called Martin Harrison who was playing for a Brum blues outfit 'The Indigo Set'. He had previously worked with Nicky James, 'The Astonaires' and 'Johnny King and the Aces'. Martin wasn't into the music and wanted to leave, Colin wanted to get back into singing. He had had a short spell with 'The Dischords' in the summer of 1965 and was keen to join a new group, so Jane put the two together. They met at the Park Attwood and got on well; they soon found a bass player, Al Attwood from Stourbridge, who had previously played for 'Buddy Britten and the Regents'. They were almost a complete group. At the same time Rob Newell and Ian Hardiman, also ex-'Zodiacs' were trying to form a band with the help of former 'Zodiacs' manager Keith Hubbard. Keith got hold of Colin, they all met at the Green Man and a new group was formed. Martin brought the name 'The Indigo Set' with him as the blues outfit had split up. Rehearsals began at the Navigation Inn in Clensmore. They had an initial set back when Rob Newell's bass gear was stolen from the Navigation. It was recovered by police but the speakers had been taken out and so new gear had to be bought. The original line up was: Colin Youngjohns-vocals, Ian Hardiman-lead guitar, Rob Newell-bass, Mick Thomas-rhythm and Martin Harrison drums. Al Atwood was at this stage surplus to requirements but turned up for rehearsals anyway. Mick Thomas only did about six gigs with them, before he left and was replaced by Al Atwood; this became the classic 'Indigo Set' line up. Their music was based on black American soul numbers, particularly Stax and Motown songs from the likes of Wilson Pickett, 'The Temptations' and 'Smokey Robinson and the Miracles'. I introduced quite a few numbers to the band being an avid soul fan, songs

by 'The Impressions' off the Big Sixteen album, Major Lance ('*Um,Um,Um*'), and Billy Stewarts '*Sitting in the Park*' being some examples. Colin was also a big fan of PJ Proby and with his large vocal range did justice to dramatic ballads like '*Maria*' and '*Hold Me*' giving 'The Indigo Set' a unique place on the group scene.

THE INDIGO SET
*at Habberley Valley.
l to r Ian Hardiman, Al Atwood, Colin Youngjohns, Rob Newell, Martin Harrison*

Keith Hubbard, their manager, started getting them plenty of work. A promoter who ran a large club in Digbeth was a big fan of the of the band and got a major agent from Wolverhampton to check them out. The result being they had plenty of work all over the Black Country, Old Hill Plaza, The Rowley Rag, The Beehive, The Caves at Walsall, The Metro and many more. At one point they played eleven consecutive nights, including three in one night. Starting at the Black Horse in Kidderminster they moved on to the Metro in Wolverhampton and finished up at the Penthouse in Birmingham. Other Birmingham venues they played were the Cedar Club (where Viv Prince, drummer of 'The Pretty Things', turned up one night and nearly demolished Martin's drum kit), the Elbow Room, where they played with 'Deep Feeling' (Jim Capaldi, Dave Mason), as Mr. '*Green Door*', Frankie Vaughan, sat in the audience. They played all the usual local gigs, the Chateau, Park Attwood, etc. and the Welsh seaside resorts in the summer, doing Up the Junction at Crewe one night and then driving straight onto Newquay; they also played Welshpool and Rhyl.

This constant gigging gave the band a great rapport, Al and Ian's backing vocals complementing Colin's voice, and for a time 'The Indigo Set' gelled into a really tight sophisticated unit. In the summer of 1967 Al Attwood broke his arm in a car accident and although he did a few gigs singing backing vocals, things weren't the same and he left shortly after. With Al gone the vocal harmonies suffered. Rob, who had always got on well with Al, was not happy with the sound and wanted a change of direction, so he announced that as soon as a replacement bass player could be found, he was leaving. They were playing at the Chateau one night when Sam Connell rhythm guitarist with Worcester group 'The Suedes' asked if he could replace Rob on bass, announcing he'd never played bass before but would soon learn if somebody taught him. Impressed by Sam's enthusiasm he got the job and Rob left; Sam went out and bought himself a bass guitar. As they were only a four piece Sam suggested they got in another ex-'Suede', guitarist Joey Dunnett, who had just recently left 'The Renegades', a group which had been very popular in Finland. He could play lead or rhythm and sing backing vocals. So Joe joined in October 1967 and they became a five piece again. But Ian wasn't happy, the group had lost direction, the tight three-part harmonies had gone, Joe and Sam were more into heavy rock, so Ian left. This was more or less the end of 'The Indigo Set'. They did a few more gigs including one supporting 'Reparata and the Delrons' at Droitwich Winter Gardens and eventually split up early in 1968. Rob Newell later on joined 'Bluesberry Hill', Colin dedicated himself to Kidderminster Harriers, while Martin Harrison left with me to go to London in the spring of 1968.

FOOTNOTE

Martin Harrison carried on as a drummer and had an interesting career, firstly joining a pop group 'The Hi Fi's' who were big in Germany. When they split up after a brief period in London, he returned to Germany (Munchen Gladbach) to join psychedelic underground band 'The Look': Werner Odenkirchen, guitar; Blackie, bass, also keyboards. This lasted a chaotic, poverty stricken year, when Martin was invited down to Munich by ex 'Hi Fi' Gary Unwin who got him session work for Ester and Abi Ofarim. Martin learnt sight reading and became a full time session musician working a lot for Giorgio Moroder in his studio in the cellar of the Arabella Hotel in Munich, drumming on three Donna Summer albums *Love To Love*

You', 'Hostage', and 'Four Seasons of Love'. He also recorded the 'Funky Family' album for 'Sister Sledge' and 'Living In A Madhouse' for 'Silver Convention' both produced by Silvester Levi. He also worked for Frank Farian drumming on most of 'Boneys M's 'Rivers of Babylon' album. He also drummed on the hit single 'Automatic Lover' by 'DeeDee' Jackson written by Gary Unwin. His work in Munich was interrupted by a brief period in London recording an experimental album for Austrian singer Bobby Heimer. The album was called 'Zacharias' and only consisted of bass and drums. Although very enjoyable to record it was a commercial failure, selling only about 200 copies.

THE INDIGO SET

New line up Oct 1967
l to r Standing
Martin Harrison
Ian Hardiman,
Joe Dunnett,
Sam Connell,
Front, Colin Youngjohns

During all his time in Germany, Martin had worked with a George Hayman kit which he had bought in London. It was copper-lined and one of a very few of its kind. But the days of real drum kits for session work finished in 1986 with the arrival of the drum machine. The phone just stopped ringing. Since then Martin has changed direction completely and he became a tennis coach in Munich. In spite of his interesting and varied career, Martin still remembers fondly his time spent in Kidderminster as the best years of his life.

THE JAVELINS
1963

Formed in 1963, they were three friends from King Charles Grammar School, Nigel 'Sam' Knowles on drums, Johnny Pasternak - guitar and Al King - vocals. They were joined by two lads from Bayton, Terry Edwards, bass and Mervyn Dyke, rhythm. Johnny Pasternak had met Mervyn Dyke when he left school and went to work at the old Stanley Goodwin garage in Worcester Road. Mervyn was a bit of an electronics wizard and helped build the bands amplification. They practised for a whole year at Bayton Village Hall before playing their first gig, Nigel having to take his drum kit all the way from Kidderminster to Bayton on the bus.

They were eventually ready for live gigs and played their first date at a summer fete at Nineveh, a mansion near Bayton owned by the Marston-Smedley family (of Smedley's canned peas). Mervyn Dyke didn't stay with the group long and was soon replaced by Roy Price. Later on the group became influenced by rhythm 'n' blues and changed their name to......

THE CRAWLING KINGSNAKES
1964 - 1965

...named after a John Lee Hooker number. They began rehearsing a new set at the Thurston Hotel in Bewdley. Sometime during this period Johnny Pasternak left to join 'The Shakedown Sound' while Al King was replaced on vocals by seventeen year old Robert Plant from Hayley Green; Ian 'Inky' Watts joined on lead guitar. 'The Kingsnakes' played the same venues as the 'Shakedown Sound' mostly on the Regan circuit and it was at Old Hill Plaza that John Bonham invited himself to take over on drums from Nigel Knowles. After further rehearsals at Clows Top Village Hall, the new line up was Robert Plant – vocals, Ian 'Inky' Watts – lead guitar, Roy Price – rhythm, Terry Edwards – bass and John Bonham – drums. They carried on gigging in the Midlands. On one occasion at the Ritz in Kings Heath, John Bonham launched his drum kit down a long flight of stairs, it was the quickest way to the van. Another time at Kidderminster Town Hall when 'The Yardbirds' played there, Ian Watts impressed Eric Clapton when he played Eric's guitar after the show. In September 1965 Inky Watts left for Newcastle University and a previous bass player 'Maverick' Oakes took over on lead.

'The Kingsnakes' carried on for a few months more, Robert Plant impressing everybody with his powerful vocals. But the group split up at the end of the year, Terry Edwards joining up with Elmer O'Shea to form Bonehead. For Robert Plant, this was just the start of a brilliant career. He joined Midlands group 'Listen' with whom he made three singles for CBS, before forming the 'Band of Joy' where he was joined by John Bonham and ex-'Shakedown' guitarist Kevyn Gammond.

*THE CRAWLING
KINGSNAKES
rehearsing at the
Thurston (Bewdley)*

*l to r:
Johnny Pasternak
(rhythm)
Nigel Knowles (Drums)
Maverick (Bass)
Ian Watts (Lead)*

Photo: Nigel Knowles

THE MONEY JUNGLE
1965 - 1968

Formed towards the end of 1965 this band was originally called 'The Astrals'. The line up was Mick Packwood, vocals; Dicky Hughes, drums; Tony Huxon, bass; Pete Downham, rhythm; and ex-'Shakedowner' Bill Davies on lead. However, this line up was short lived and they soon changed singers, with ex-'Crawling Kingsnake' Al King taking over from Mick Packwood. With the change of vocalist came a new name, 'The Money Jungle'. Rehearsing at the Mare and Colt, Bill Davies had his Watkin Rapier stolen, so Kevyn Gammond lent Bill his Zenith with DeArmond pick-up on a more or less permanent basis. The band had some luck with equipment. They were also loaned a Park PA system by Rodney Simmonds (ex-'Cruisers'), which they also kept on a permanent basis. 'Money Jungle' used to play the Ma Regan circuit regularly, including the Adelphi at West

Bromwich, which had a revolving stage; due to a lack of foresight when the stage came round their drum kit fell right off the edge; the audience loved it, assuming 'Money Jungle' were a comedy outfit. Acts that they supported at the Plazas were 'The Herd', 'The Lovin Spoonful', Lulu and the original 'Drifters'. They also supported 'Screamin' Lord Sutch' at Kidderminster Town Hall.

In 1967 Al King left and was replaced by Butch Humber (ex-'Huskies') who brought along with him 'The Huskies' Bill Simmonds on drums, who replaced Dicky Hughes.

'Money Jungle' split up early in 1968, Bill Davies later moving on to play with 'Runyard Smith' and then 'Hardpad'.

NORMAN'S CONQUESTS
1967

A short lived rock 'n'roll revival group, Norman's Conquests were: Norman Clarke - vocals, Mick Worsap - guitar, Dave Holder - bass, Malcolm Shore - rhythm, and Dave Bodley -drums. Dave Holder and Dave Bodley went on to form "Censored with ex-'Invader 'Dave Tiplady.

THE RAIDERS
1962 - 1964

'The Raiders' were originally a skiffle group formed by a bunch of lads living in the Hall Street, Clensmore Area. They were 'Tisser' Rollins – vocals, Tony Goodman – drums and washboard, and Dave Beckley – bass. They used to rehearse in the outhouse of The Royal George run by Rob Newells' uncle. Rob, inspired by his older brother's Eddie Cochran and Gene Vincent records, used to practise on Dave Beckley's Antoria bass which he used to leave in the rehearsal room. When Mick Thomas and Colin Hepwood, rhythm and lead guitar respectively, joined up, they suggested that Rob Newell take on the bass, partly because he was keen but also he looked a bit like Heinz. No sooner said than done, with Rob on bass, Dave Beckley left, his two mates 'Tisser' Rollins and Tony Goodman soon following. A very young Jess Roden was watching 'The Raiders' with friends at St Mary's Youth Club. With shouts of "I can sing this better", Jess jumped on stage and joined the group singing 'Shakin All Over'. He became their vocalist there and then, with Chris Hayes taking over on drums. This line-up remained the same until 1964 when they split up.

'The Raiders' played all the local venues such as the SDF Club where Rob had to rescue his newly bought Fender Precision bass which was spinning violently around on stage, knocked down by a careless punter. Other venues included the local village halls and Frank Freeman's, which also became their base and rehearsal rooms. Later on they had support spots at Kidderminster Town Hall, with 'The Hollies', Tom Jones and 'Twinkle', who was found lying on her back in the dressing room eating a raw onion. Other great support slots at the Town Hall were 'The Yardbirds' with Eric Clapton on lead guitar, and 'The Small Faces'. When Ronnie Lane's bass amp broke down, he borrowed Rob Newell's. They also had other support slots to major acts at Stourbridge Town Hall and Old Hill Plaza.

They split up in 1964, Jess had been interested in doing more blues orientated material and got the chance when he joined 'The Sunsetters' after vocalist Alfie Knott had left them. Colin and Nick wanted to do more commercial material and Rob wanted to continue with rock based music, so he joined up with 'The Zodiacs'.

THE RAIDERS
 at Frank Freeman's
Back Row l to r:
Rob Newell
Mick Thomas
Colin Hepwood
Front:
Chris Hayes
Jess Roden
manager Norris Cale

THE SCORPIONS
1963 - 1967

Bob Barber had his first guitar lessons with Mildred Owens in her small studio at the top of Swan Street. He also learnt violin and piano there. A lot of youngsters used to take in sheet music of Lonnie Donegan skiffle songs, as Mildred used to teach them how to play chords and how to keep time by beating the rhythm out with a stick. Bob later became a biker and used to hang around the Flamingo cafe. It was there he met Jim Boden who wanted to form a band. Bob wanted to be the singer, Jim was a guitarist and knew another guitarist, John Gwilliam, who could play bass, and also a drummer from Kinver, Martin Hill, who had played with the 'Revniks'. Martin's father Stan, a builder, offered to manage the band, so calling themselves

THE SCORPIONS

l to r Jim Boden, Martin Hill, Bob Barber, John Gwilliam
Photo: Duckworth Wood

'The Scorpions' they were ready to start. A local farmer, Mr Fernihough, sponsored their stage clothes, which were pale grey suits; they became known as 'Scorpion' suits. They did lots of work in the Black Country, the Park Attwood, Black Horse, the Chateau, Droitwich Winter Gardens and the SDF club and came second to 'Tommy and the Crestas' in a beat ompetition in Quarry Bank. Towards the end of 'The Scorpions' they changed drummers, Martin Hill being essentially a dance band drummer, (he did a great Gene Krupa style solo). Martin left and was replaced by Jim Boden's cousin Dave Smith.

During this time Bob had bumped into Graham Drew on his insurance round. Graham was guitarist in 'The Reflections' and told Bob they were looking for a singer. He lent Bob a couple of records to learn, which he sang at the audition. Bob passed the audition easily and joined 'The Reflections'. This signalled the end of 'The Scorpions'.

THE SIMONALS
1963 - 1964

'The Simonals' were formed in March 1963, and must have been the youngest group around at the time. Rhythm guitarist Phil Chadbourne (ex-'Strangers Incorporated'), was the oldest at fifteen and a half, Ian Simmonds - lead guitar, Chris Connelly - vocals, and Rob Elcock - drums, were all fourteen. Initially they were managed by Rob's father, Arthur, and later on by Ian's father, Fred who was nephew to the butcher Sid Simmonds. Arthur Elcock got them a couple of auditions for the ATV television company in Birmingham, the winner of one of them was 'Denny Laine and the Diplomats'. In September 1963 they won a pop group competition at Stourport Carnival, narrowly beating 'The Raiders' into second place. In January 1964 they came second in a National Beat Competition at the Locarno in Birmingham, the prize was a support spot to the 'Dave Clarke Five' at the Mecca Ballroom, Basildon. Other supports for 'The Simonals' were John Leyton, 'The Spotnicks', 'The Eagles' (from Bristol) and 'The Yardbirds'. A week after the Locarno they won another beat contest at Malvern Winter Gardens, beating nine other groups into top place. Early in 1964 bassist Rob Newell joined 'The Simonals' after 'The Raiders' had split up. In August that year they came second in a talent competition at the Far Forest Show. By the end of the year 'The Simonals' days were drawing to a close, as they wanted to experiment with other types of music. They split up in December 1964. Rob Newell joined 'The Zodiacs' and later 'The Indigo Set', Ian joined 'The Profits' (formerly 'The Huskies'), Chris Connelly later joined the 'Crestas' when Tommy Noyes left. Rob Elcock joined 'The Montanas' a very popular group at the time from Wolverhampton, and also had a spell with 'Sounds of Blue'.

THE SIMONALS
at the Black Horse 1964.
l to r. Ian Simmonds,
Rob Elcock, Chris Connelly, Phil
Chadbourne, Rob Newell

STRANGERS INCORPORATED
1963

'Strangers Incorporated' could be said to be Stan Webb's first group. Stan one of the UK's leading blues guitarists was born and brought up in Fulham, south west London. In 1959 at the age of thirteen he moved to Kidderminster with his family, settling in   Drakes Crescent on the Habberley Estate. He went to the local school, Harry Cheshire, and was soon involved in the school skiffle group, 'The Cheshire Cats' with whom he sometimes played tea chest bass or guitar along with school friends Paul Turner – guitar, Tim Jackson – drums, and Mike Preston – keyboards. On a couple of occasions they had spots on the same bill as Tim's elder brother Roger (who later became keyboard player with 'The Tornados'). This led to Stan, along with Tim, joining one of Roger Jackson's groups in 1960 called 'The Blue Four'. The line up was Roger Jackson – piano, Stan Webb – guitar, Tim Jackson – drums, and Mike Davies – vocals. They were supplemented by three girl vocalists, the Rowberry sisters from Wolverley. They played regularly at the Fountain and also had gigs at the TA Drill Hall in Stourport, and an RAF camp in Bridgnorth.

This experience encouraged Stan to form his own band, 'Strangers Incorporated', at the end of 1962. With Stan on lead were: Ivan Phipps,bass; Phil Chadbourne, rhythm; and Roger Darby, drums. They did a lot of instrumental covers like 'Czardas' by 'Nero and the Gladiators', 'Golden Earring' by 'Dave Sampson and the Hunters' and also numbers by 'Mike Berry and the Outlaws'. Stan liked to avoid all the obvious numbers by 'The Shadows' that everybody else was doing. They played all the regular venues like St. Mary's Hall, the SDF club, Frank Freeman's and the Boar's Head in Worcester Street, where they played at a Tramps Supper. In March 1963 they had a residency at the Central Cinema, opening up before the main film, 'Summer Holiday', starring Cliff Richard. For this week they had a singer called Barney who sang some of the songs from the film. Unfortunately on the first show he forgot to switch his mic on (an Italian Gelloso), until prompted by Stan shouting 'switch the mic on'! The group drifted apart during the summer of 1963 so Stan went about forming a new group.

At the time Stan was working at the Kidderminster Times in Bridge Street.. Rae Spencer was also working there and Stan asked him if he wanted to join a band. Rae jumped at the chance and joined on rhythm guitar, his brother Alvar joining on drums with a kit his dad helped him to buy from Jones and Crossland in Birmingham. Just around the corner from the Times office was Rogersons men's clothes shop in Oxford Street, where old school friend Paul Turner worked. He was soon roped in on bass. Completing the line-up was another old friend of Stan's, Roger Sullivan. Stan accompanied a somewhat sceptical Roger up to Birmingham where they bought a couple of harmonicas in the keys of G and B flat. So the band was formed, calling themselves.........

SHADES FIVE

1963 - 1965

THE

SHADES

5

back row l to r: Rae Spencer, Alvar Spencer, Roger Sullivan Front Row l to r:. Stan Webb, Paul Turner.

Rehearsals began in the autumn of 1963, above the Spencers café on Severnside North, Bewdley. The Spencer's had originally ran Teddy Gray's ice cream and sweet shop on the other side of the bridge. While looking through the records for sale during one of his frequent trips to the Diskery in Birmingham, he came across the likes of Muddy Waters and 'Howlin Wolf'. Stan particularly liked the swing and depth to original American blues. They acquired a manager in John Carter and started gigging extensively. For a while they had a residency at the Green Man, they also did the Ma Regan circuit, the Brum Kavern and various support spots at Kidderminster and Stourbridge Town Halls to the likes of 'Freddy and the Dreamers' and 'The Hollies' and a memorable gig at Cadbury Social Club supporting the legendary American rocker Gene Vincent. They also played further afield at venues such as The Gaff at Banbury, the Twisted Wheel, Manchester and the Three Coins, Leeds. Sometimes the sequence of gigs was far from ideal, on one occasion Alvar having to drive the van from Skegness to Aberystwyth, an eleven-hour journey in those days. Nearer to home they played a couple of Saturday

SHADES FIVE
live at Kidderminster
Town Hall
left Rae Spencer
right Stan Webb

morning spots at the Central Cinema for the ABC minors. Paul Turner was not allowed to play, as his boss at Rogersons, Cliff Horton, wouldn't give him the time off. On the second Saturday he decided to take a chance, but was caught red-handed by Cliff carrying equipment into the cinema. "Traddin' again eh", Cliff said to Paul,   "Pick up your cards on Monday". So ended Paul Turner's job at Rogersons.

After this gig at the Central, the band headed straight to London for a recording session arranged by Phil Solomon, who had spotted them at the Brum Kavern. They first did an audition in a cellar studio in Denmark Street, then recorded four numbers in Decca's Studio in Lansdowne Road, Notting Hill. Two were self-penned by Stan, the others were a Chuck Berry and a Bo Diddley number. Acetates were pressed and John Carter sent them away, but nothing more was heard of them.

Music wasn't the only thing that was important: the clothes and the look had to be right. Stan remembers wearing Paisley shirts with tab collars, leather waistcoats and trousers, Cuban heel boots, as worn by 'The Beatles', supplied by Anello and David of London courtesy of Mr Blunt of Blunt's shoes. Stan and Paul virtually used to stop the traffic as they walked through town. In fact Stan's clothes were a source of trouble at Carpet Trades where his dad had got him a job in the stock records department on the top floor. I was working there at the time along with the other lads in our regulation suits. We were pretty impressed by his gear, but not so the floor manager who called Stan into his office everyday. But the warnings didn't work, in spite of his father's efforts, Stan's one and only burning ambition was to become a professional musician. Other temporary jobs Stan had included Pycock and Wicket the photographers, and Josiah Stallards the wine merchants. Anyway, the group had been promised work in Germany at Studio 44 in Munchen Gladbach in the summer of 1964, so Stan was quite happy to leave Carpet Trades in the spring of that year. Publicity photos had been taken and passports and ferry tickets ordered when the bad news came through that Rae Spencer couldn't go, as he was only sixteen, so the German trip was cancelled. Sometime after this the band met Harry Lawrence, a DJ at the Whisky-a-Go-Go in Birmingham. He started turning up to the 'Shades Five' gigs and began influencing the group. This was not to Stan's liking, Harry was turning the group in a direction Stan

Back stage at the Central l to r: Stan Webb, Rae Spencer, Alvar Spencer, Roger Sullivan

didn't believe in. He had always had a lot of faith in the band but following recent disappointments Harry's appearance on the scene was the final straw. Stan left the band and Harry took over on vocals and keyboard.

Things went well from the beginning. Although John Carter had finished as manager they were getting work from the Billy Forester Agency, and money had been invested in new stage clothes. At the Flamingo in Wardour Street they supported 'Zoot Money and his Big Roll Band' when Eric Burdon came rushing in from the Marquee and announced on stage that *'House Of The Rising Sun'* had just reached number one in the charts. Also in the Flamingo that night was David Hogg from the J Walter Thompson Agency who thought they would be ideal to appear in a commercial they wanted to film advertising Kellogg's Corn Flakes. The shoot took place at Lord Baths palace at Longleat in Wiltshire. It was a great week's fun for the band, who got £75 each for their troubles. They had written a Bo Diddley style riff, which in the end was recorded by session musicians. The band themselves were turned into animated characters in a cartoon and plans were made to call 'Shades Five' – 'The Gonks'. Nothing ever came of this, probably just as well!

They gigged extensively throughout 1965 supporting the likes of 'The Kinks' and Gene Pitney. But their health had deteriorated, life on the road was quite tough, the cheques often bounced and they were often reduced to sleeping in the van and nicking pies from the transport cafes. So, in spite of the offer of a lucrative residency at the newly opened Metro Club in Birmingham, they had had enough and decided to call it a day; this was towards the end of 1965. Paul Turner went on to join Cliff Ward (Martin Rayner) for a while and was also involved with John Carter running the famous all-nighters at The Chateau.

SOUNDS OF BLUE
1964 - 1965

Andy Silvester came from Hackman's Gate, a hamlet about a mile outside the village of Blakedown where his father owned the village grocery store. Andy played the banjo in a trad jazz band 'The Fourstone Jazzmen' along with David 'Rowdy' Yeats on vocals, Derek Tew on trumpet, Pete 'Clunky' Chapman on clarinet and Ed Davis on drums. When this band split in the late spring of 1964, Andy and Rowdy decided to form a rhythm 'n' blues group.

THE FOURSTONE JAZZMEN
bottom left: Rowdy Yeats   bottom centre: Andy Silvester

They often socialised in the pubs of Stourbridge, particularly in The Turf, but it was in the Spotted Cow that they arranged to meet Chris Wood. That very night Christine Perfect was playing the piano. Both Chris Wood and Christine joined the band, Chris Wood on sax and flute while Christine started off by playing bass. They were looking for a guitarist and Stan Webb came immediately to mind. Andy had followed 'Shades Five' around, as his sister Lyn used to go out with their manager John Carter, and they often picked him up in Blakedown on the way to gigs in Birmingham. So one night Andy and Rowdy went to Kidderminster Town Hall where they knew Stan was playing with 'Shades Five'.

After the gig Rowdy approached Stan outside the Town Hall and asked him if he would like to join a blues band. This was at the time when Stan had become fed up with 'Shades Five', so he willingly agreed and 'Sounds of Blue' was formed. The line up was David 'Rowdy' Yeats, vocals; Stan Webb, lead guitar; Andy Silvester, rhythm; Christine Perfect, bass; and Chris Wood, sax and flute. Initially the drummer was Roger Bruton, but he also played in a trad jazz band and often was not available. Ed Davis used to deputise until Rob Elcock (ex 'Simonals') joined them on a more or less permanent basis. On the odd occasion when they had access to a piano, Christine took it over and Phil Lawless played bass. In a way 'Sounds of Blue' were an enigma: although they built up quite a reputation they didn't actually play that many gigs. They had a residency at Dudley Liberal Club every Sunday where they had a strong following, but apart from that just a couple of gigs on the Ma Regan circuit and a couple at The Chateau were the extent of the band's gigging. Their sound was basically blues orientated; Stan remembers doing Mose Allison's, 'Parchman Farm' and Andy remembers singing 'Young Fashioned Ways' by Muddy Waters. A couple of days after a rather disappointing gig at Dudley Liberal Club, Rowdy announced he was leaving the band and as he owned most of the equipment, 'Sounds of Blue' split up; this was in March 1965. Chris Wood was great friends with the 'Spencer Davis Group' and eventually joined 'Traffic', Rowdy went to work full time at his record shop, The Groove in Stourbridge, while Christine moved down to Swanage in Dorset and got a job as a chambermaid at the Grosvenor Hotel, together with her

Record store bag preserved and loaned by Andy Silvester.

friend Sheila. From there she wrote to Andy asking him and the gang to come down and visit her, complaining that the music scene in Swanage was pretty poor but that Bournemouth was good, when they could get there. She mentioned midnight walks on the beach and playing Miles Davis records back in her room. When Andy eventually replied that he was coming down with Paul Turner, Christine wrote to him to meet her and Sheila at the Pier Head café with instructions to "Be sure to wear your best gear, since you're friends of mine from the Midlands; must impress them you know"! So Andy and Paul drove down to Swanage in the Silvester family grocery van. Paul remembers wearing a Blue Beat trilby hat with a blue V-neck leather slipover.

Letter sent by Christine Perfect to Andy Silvester from Swanage

They all went off to the Disco-a-Go-Go in Bournemouth where Andy heard for the first time Otis Redding, Wilson Pickett and 'Jnr. Walker and the Allstars' blasting out at full volume (on record). Andy was totally knocked out by the new Stax sound and the weird dances the mods were doing. Back at Hackman's Gate, Stan had virtually moved in, Lyn Silvester was now his girlfriend. This was a relatively inactive period for Stan and Andy, were socialising round the clubs, listening to new records and trying out new numbers in the laundry at the rear of the house which they used as a rehearsal room. But they were determined to start a new group and when they found out that Alan Morley, drummer with 'The Redcaps' was free, they contacted him immediately. 'The Redcaps' were a well-known Birmingham outfit who had had records released including a great version of Chuck Berry's *Talkin 'Bout You*; Andy in particular liked the drum fill Alan Morley had played in it. 'The Redcaps' had been virtually a resident group at the two Regan Plazas and Andy and Stan knew them well. Anyway, Alan teamed up with them and a trio was formed which eventually became ....

CHICKEN SHACK

1966 -

Their first recorded gig was on New Year's Eve 1966 at the Ritz in Kings Heath. They also played an all-nighter at the Chateau on January 20th, 1967, where they used, for the first time, newly acquired Marshall stacks. They were LOUD, so loud in fact that they were asked to turn down the volume at the Mews in Moseley as they were literally rattling the glasses off the tables and shelves. On the 22nd February they did an audition at Digbeth for EMI but were classified 'as not commercial enough'! Four days later they met Mike Vernon at Rowdy Yeats Groove record shop in Stourbridge. Rowdy knew Mike Vernon through the shop and tipped the group off that Mike was looking for new talent for a blues label he was starting up called Blue Horizon. So the band sent Mike some tapes which a few weeks previously had been recorded in the laundry room with a tape recorder borrowed from Andy's girlfriend of the time, Sylvia. Although of poor quality Mike Vernon was suitably impressed by what he heard and followed the group back to Hackman's Gate where he sat in on their rehearsal in the laundry room, fresh plaster on the walls (Stan and Andy were temporarily working as builders labourers at the time and the plaster from the site came in handy). Mike liked what he heard and a recording session was arranged to do some proper demo tapes. It was during this trip to the Midlands that Mike Vernon discovered Jeremy Spencer who was playing in a Lichfield group called 'The Levi Set' at the time.

During this period Christine Perfect had moved to London and was working as a window dresser at Dickens and Jones in Regent Street. The group thought they were a bit limited as a trio and had been trying to contact her; eventually reaching her through one of their drinking friends from The Turf pub, actor Mike Lewis. Christine was interested and came up to meet them at the Mews in Moseley where the group were playing. Liking what she heard, Christine decided to renew her musical career and when the band went down to London on April 14th to buy some clothes and meet her, Christine told them she had handed her notice in at Dickens and Jones and was heading back to the Midlands to join them. This, as it turned out later, was a momentous decision, which would eventually lead her to worldwide fame and fortune.

Back in the Midlands things moved fast. Through Colin Parsons of the Mews at Moseley they were put in touch with the ADSELL Agency who had an office just off the Five Ways in Birmingham. They were in touch with a certain Henry Henroid who was Gene Vincent's manager. Based in Hamburg he often scouted for new acts in Britain to play at the legendary Star Club. So the deal was done: 'Chicken Shack' were to play the Star Club. There followed a quick dash down to London for Christine to get her passport. Alan Morley drove her down, and it was during this trip that Alan met Christine's friend Jill, who was a fellow window dresser at Dickens and Jones. It was one of those lucky meetings, as Jill eventually became Alan's wife.

So at the beginning of June, Jim Conway, their roadie, and another drinking pal from The Turf, turned up in a battered old Morris J2 van outside the Silvester house in Hackman's Gate. Andy's dad took one look at it and said "Never mind Hamburg - I wouldn't go to Blakedown in that." Anyway they caught the ferry at Hull all right and arrived in Hamburg on Friday 5th June 1967. They had the weekend free and began work on Monday June 8th. On the same bill were 'The Sound of Syke' and the 'Boston Show Band'. The schedule was punishing, the show kicking off at 7pm through to about 3am the following morning, sometimes even including a late afternoon performance at 4pm for the youngsters. They played about an hour at a time alternating with the other groups. The last hour was reserved for records when the bands could sit down, relax and share a chat with the working girls who had just arrived after their night's work entertaining the public. Booze and dope were obviously available in copious amounts, but to keep awake you needed 'uppers', the trouble with these being that they worked too well. Andy recalls one day heading off to the beach after a full night's work and not returning to the club until the evening to start playing again, compounding the lack of sleep problem. There was never any shortage of female company. Apart from the regular customers that came to watch the groups, the strippers and prostitutes would also be amenable and be your girlfriend during your stay in Hamburg. Christine also had a bit of a fling with the German bass player in Tony Sheridan's band, 'Volke'. She was less keen however on the attentions of Hilda, the lesbian manageress and singer around Hamburg, who used to leave love notes for Christine on her piano. Andy liked one of the working girls who came to the club, but decided that dreams of taking her back to Hackman's Gate was probably not a sensible idea. But another of the girls, Monica, used to scare the hell out of Andy after she transferred her attentions to him. Andy looked quite similar to one of the 'Remo Four', with whom Monica had just finished a tempestuous affair by throwing all his clothes out of an upstairs window on to the street. Another scary person there was resident English rocker Tony Sheridan who spotted a black belt

Andy was wearing when they were drinking in the bar next door to the Star Club. Andy had two of these belts obtained from a cobbler in Cradley Heath recommended by Chris Wood's sister Stephanie, fashion designer for the group. Tony Sheridan said, "I like that", Andy explained to him that he couldn't have it, whereupon Tony said, "I want it". Volke the bass player whispered in Andy's ear, "You had better give it to him." A compromise was reached and Andy gave Tony his spare brown one. In spite of this, Andy was an admirer of Tony Sheridan's guitar playing, particularly in a Jimmy Reed number *'Baby What Do You Want Me To Do?'*, better known as *'Peepin' and Hidin'*. Christine also loved this number: it had a great groove with a Hammond organ riff running through it. This month of excess and hard work came to an end on July 5th when 'Chicken Shack' left Hamburg and arrived safely home at Hackman's Gate in the old J2, weary and much more worldly wise.

On their return Mike Vernon had been busy getting dates for them at classic London rock venues like Klooks Kleek, the Marquee, Cooks Ferry Inn and the Fishmongers Arms in Wood Green. They began commuting between London and Worcestershire sometimes staying at Mike Vernon's mansion flat in Finchley and sometimes at Stan's grandparents house in Brookville Road, Fulham. Immediately on their return Christine bought an electric piano, a Hofner Pianette. Their big break came when Mike Vernon

Rehearsing at the Nags Head, Battersea.
l to r Christine Perfect, Stan Webb, Andy Silvester, Al Sykes

got them a spot at Windsor Jazz Festival on Sunday August 13th with a host of other acts like Elton John and 'Bluesology' and future Blue Horizon stable mates Peter Green's 'Fleetwood Mac'. They were playing in the

marquee on the night session when Stan bust a string during the set. Peter Green, who had been watching from the side lent Stan his guitar. They had a chat afterwards and Peter Green complimented Stan on his playing. Further London club dates followed including the Marquee with 'Fleetwood Mac' and Eel Pie Island with Champion Jack Dupree, and an appearance at the Saville Theatre on 17th September along with John Mayall, 'Fleetwood Mac' and 'The Aynsley Dunbar Retaliation'. Sometime during this period Alan Morley left and was temporary replaced by Hughie Flint who had previously drummed with John Mayall. This didn't last long and when Mike Vernon, through the Rik Gunnel Agency, got 'Chicken Shack' the job of backing Freddy King on his UK tour, Al Sykes took over the drummer's role, as the band already knew Al from their stint at the Star Club. When Freddy came over they had their first rehearsal at the Ram Jam club in Brixton, running through 'CC Baby', Freddy had a big grin on his face and said "Man we don't need no rehearsal". This was due to the fact that Andy and Stan had bought the LP 'Freddy King Sings' on one of their frequent visits to the Diskery in Birmingham and had learnt practically every number on the album. Freddy also admired Christine's piano playing, which was very much in the style of Sonny Thompson, Freddy's manager/pianist.

The Freddy King tour kicked off on the 6th October at the Cricketer's Inn, Southend. The tour was a great success and a real learning curve for the band. They used to do a warm up spot of their own before Freddy took over the spotlight. He had a great rapport with fellow American Al Syke, one of Al's party pieces being a drum solo using the rings on his fingers as drumsticks. Freddy King was not only a fine guitarist but a useful mechanic as well; he cleaned out the carburettor one night when their battered old J2 van broke down. On October 15th they played the Saville Theatre again, on the same bill was 'Jnr Walker and the All-stars'. The tour wound up at the Queen Elizabeth College, East London on Saturday October 21st. On the way to the gig, the van stopped and Andy asked directions in his best middle-class English accent "Excuse me, can you tell me the way to Mile End Road?" This cracked Freddy up completely and kept him amused all the way to the venue. After the tour Al Syke returned to the States, so 'Chicken Shack' took on another drummer. Judy Vernon knew somebody from Kingston-on-Thames, Dave Bidwell who had previous played in 'The Muskrats' with Peter Green. When Dave played on the audition the general consensus was that he wasn't up to the job. Mike Vernon and Christine didn't want him in the band, but Stan liked him, he liked the way Dave swung, always an important factor in Stan's opinion. Stan said "He swings and he will get better". So Dave Bidwell joined as 'Chicken Shack's fourth drummer and stayed with them throughout their recording career with Blue Horizon. Andy remembers when he first joined he would only play the shuffle beat with his right hand on the cymbal, Andy taught him to play it two-handed, to make a more driving beat.

On the 6th December 1967, 'Chicken Shack' recorded their first single for Blue Horizon. The A-side was a Christine Perfect song ' *It's Ok With Me Baby*'. with Stan singing a Willie Dixon song, "*When My Left Eye Jumps*" on the B-side. The single was released on the 19th January 1968.

We will take our leave of 'Chicken Shack' now and meet up with them in Chapter 3, at the start of their recording career with Blue Horizon.

THE STRINGBEATS
1962 – 1965

This group is not be confused with the popular soul band from Birmingham who had the same name. These 'Stringbeats' came from Stourport, they were formed in 1962 and played mainstream rock and pop. The line up was: Terry Chandler,lead guitar and vocals; Charlie Bullock,rhythm guitar and vocals; Roger Capewell, bass; and Dave MacAulay, drums. They rehearsed at the Walshes Tenants Hall and also in Terry Chandler's back room. Both his parents were very supportive, in fact they managed the band. The usual round of gigs followed, their first was at the SDF social club. They also played the Green Man, the Nautical William, Frank Freeman's, the Black Horse and a host of Black Country clubs after passing an audition at Alveley Social Club. In August 1964 they came third in a talent contest at the Far Forest Show, just behind 'The Simonals'. They then entered an audition at Blackpool Winter Gardens for the chance to play in Germany. Although they passed the audition and were offered work abroad, parental misgivings about the whole enterprise stopped the group from taking up the offer. Shortly after this Terry Chandler left the band to try his luck elsewhere and the group folded.

THE SUNSETTERS
1962 – 1963

'The Sunsetters' were formed in 1962 by ex 'Crestas' vocalist Alfie Knott. They rehearsed at Worcester Cross Youth Club. The original line up was Alfie Knott vocals, Terry Clarke on lead guitar, Dave Pugh, his friend from Sebright School on bass, Phil Chadbourne on rhythm, and Sean Jenkins on drums. They played the usual village halls and clubs in the area, knocking out rock 'n' roll numbers by people like Elvis Presley and Gene Vincent. Gene Vincent was a great inspiration to Alfie who modelled his stage act and persona on the American rocker, to the extent of copying Gene's limp by dragging his leg behind him. Towards the end of the year Alfie thought a change of name might do the band good, so for a while they were called 'Alfie Knott and the AK's'. It didn't help a lot as shortly after Terry Clarke left to join 'Cliff Ward's Cruisers'. The others soon followed and the band folded, although Sean Jenkins stayed with him.

Alfie didn't hang around long and 'The Sunsetters' mark 2 was soon up and running. He had remembered a very young guitarist, Kevyn Gammond, from the early days of the 'Crestas'. Kevyn also remembered Alfie very well, as he had played his first ever gig with Alfie and 'The Crestas' in 1961. This was at Stourport Town Hall, it made a great impression on Kevyn at the time. As soon as the set kicked off, Alfie went berserk, leering and twitching, hips grinding, legs vibrating, his hair hanging over his forehead. The boys all stood around the edge of the dance hall, trying to look cool with their brylcreemed hair, draped jackets and winkle-picker shoes, the girls down the front, dancing round their handbags. The look was very important, no more were teenagers dressed like miniature versions of their parents, although it could be hard work and get you into trouble, sitting in the bath with your jeans on to get them real tight; Kevyn was often sent home from school because of his clothes and hairstyle. This night however finished early for Kevyn, his mum and dad picked him up at 9.30 pm as he was still at school; they didn't really approve of the band, although they liked the fact he was taking part in youth club activities. As for 'The Crestas', they needed somebody who could play to the end of the show and soon got in Dave Mansfield on rhythm guitar.

So Kevyn enthusiastically joined up with Alfie and Sean Jenkins bringing in his friend Pete Waldron on bass. Pete's bass guitar was in fact a Hofner acoustic with the slots on the neck filed bigger to fit the bass strings in. With Bill Davies on rhythm guitar, the new 'Sunsetters' line up was complete.

The group were a bit rough and ready, but Alfie rehearsed them quickly as there were bookings to fulfil. In spite of this the band looked smart on stage as Alfie insisted they wore a uniform of white shirts, red ties, black cavalry twill trousers, topped off with white acrylic 'V' neck jumpers. Their set was based on classic rock 'n' roll numbers, a few 'doo wop' songs by Frankie Lymon and the Teenagers and instrumentals by groups like 'The Ventures' and 'Duane Eddy'. Transport was supplied by Bill Davies' J2 van. A few good support spots came up for the 'Sunsetters', supporting 'Russ Sainty and the Nu Notes' and 'Screamin' Lord Sutch' at Kidderminster Town Hall. The band split up early in 1964. Alfie was the band's mentor and was like an older brother to the others, but times were changing, new influences were coming in. Pete Waldron had introduced the band to Bob Dylans music, as he had borrowed Dylan's first LP from his next door neighbour Brian Torode, who had imported it directly from the States. The material was traditional American songs sung in Bob Dylan's raw vocal style. This album and the new black music from America and the new beat groups like 'The Beatles' and 'The Stones' and all the new fashions, made 'The Sunsetters' seem old fashioned. Alfie a staunch rock 'n' roller was having none of it, so the band went one way and Alfie the other.

THE SHAKEDOWN SOUND
1964 - 1966

Kevyn and Sean were asked by Colin Youngjohns to join 'The Zodiacs', after they got up and played with them one night at Brintons club. Colin introduced Kevyn as a "young man who plays like the devil". However Kevyn did not join 'The Zodiacs', they were too mainstream for him, so they carried on minus Alfie as a four piece, changing their name to the 'Shakedown Sound', chosen by Sean Jenkins; a shakedown apparently being some kind of sofa used in the Southern States of America. At this stage with Bill Davies in the band, their set was a mixture of rock 'n' roll and blues. Although Bill didn't stay too long with them, he did play a gig with the band at the famous 2 'I's coffee bar in Soho, although nothing came out of the gig. Bill left shortly after and was replaced by Johnny Pasternak. They still needed a front man/vocalist so they invited Jess Roden from 'The Raiders' along to a gig they were doing at the Ritz in Kings Heath. Jess liked the band and auditioned for them singing Buddy Guy's *The First Time I Met The Blues*. Jess put his heart and soul into the number and passed the audition with flying colours. The 'Shakedowns' line up was now complete.

Better gigs starting coming, regular venues for the 'Shakedowns' included the Elbow Room in Birmingham where they were often watched by fellow Midlands musicians Stevie Winwood, Jim Capaldi and Dave Mason who later went on to form 'Traffic'. The Whiskey-a-Go-Go, also in Birmingham was a good gig for the band where they often backed and supported various blues artists such as T-Bone Walker, Buddy Guy, Little Walter and Screamin' Jay Hawkins, the legendary piano player who had a big U.S hit with '*I Put A Spell On You*' and whose stage act included rising from a coffin, later to be imitated by 'Screamin' Lord Sutch'.

THE SHAKEDOWNS
 in Piccadilly Circus before the 2'I's
gig
l to r:. Pete Waldron, Sean Jenkins,
Kevyn Gammond, Kneeling. Bill
Davies

When 'Screamin' Jay' turned up on the night with his manager, the manager handed over a copy of his LP and said, "Learn the set from that". They had less than an hour to rehearse it. When 'Screamin' Jay' came on stage for his show he looked a bit dubious about this bunch of young teenagers who were going to back him, his instructions were, "Don't worry, I'll telegraph the changes to you". It wasn't too bad, the great man only did a thirty-minute set anyway.

By now the 'Shakedowns' were getting really busy sometimes doing four or five gigs a night in the Birmingham area, starting at one of Ma Regan's Plazas, possibly Birmingham Town Hall, followed up by the Cavern at

Small Heath and finishing off at an all-nighter at the Whiskey. The Malcolm Rose agency in London took 'The Shakedown Sound' on and Mick Walker from 'The Redcaps' started to put the band on package tours. One memorable gig they did was at Great Yarmouth playing support to 'The Rolling Stones', the 'Walker Brothers', 'Lulu and the Lovers' and Marianne Faithfull, some line up! Other good gigs for the 'Shakedowns' were a club in Hull, The Gaff in Banbury and the famous Riki Tik Club in Windsor. Pete was earning more money from playing than from working in the wages department of Woodward Grosvenors. However he had to complete his college course and couldn't do both so he left the band. Johnny Pasternak moved over to bass and turned out a top class bass player.

After supporting 'The Who' and 'The Small Faces', the 'Shakedowns' attracted a fanatical mod following. Their repertoire now contained black inspired rhythm and blues, early soul and Tamla, and with the addition of Kevyn's 'off-the-wall' feedback-meganoise, the band developed their own distinctive style. One of Kevyn's favourite tricks was fixing bottle caps to the sole of his boots and stamping on the band's cheap co-axial cable to create an extra rhythmic sound.

Towards the end of 1966 Jess Roden left the group to join London-based soul outfit 'The Alan Bown Set'. They had spotted him at the Silver Blades in Birmingham; the 'Shakedowns' were supporting Alan Bown that night. It was a great opportunity for Jess to turn pro and move to London. Without Jess the band decided to call it a day, their equipment had nearly all been trashed due to excessive gigging and their wild stage act. Kevyn joined 'Cliff Ward's Cruisers' for a few months, he used to play 'T-Bone Shufflee' by T-Bone Walker and persuaded Cliff to sing a couple of Paul Butterfield numbers. Cliff's comment on Kevyn was "With him in the band we don't need a rhythm player". Eventually Kevyn joined Jimmy Cliff ('The Harder They Come, The Harder They Fall') a popular soul / reggae singer who was with Island Records at the time. Johnny Pasternak moved to Birmingham and Sean Jenkins joined Welsh outfit 'Eyes of Blue' who had won the Melody Maker group contest in 1965.

JIMMY CLIFF AND THE SHAKEDOWN SOUND
(with Kevyn Gammond and Sean Jenkins)
1966 - 1967

After a short spell with 'Cliff Ward and the Cruisers', in the summer of 1966, Kevyn Gammond answered an advert in the Melody Maker for musicians to back a Jamaican reggae singer, Jimmy Cliff, who Chris Blackwell had brought over to England to record on his Island label. Kevyn went down to London with fellow 'Shakedowner' Sean Jenkins, who had spent a very brief period drumming for Welsh group 'Eyes of Blue'. Both Kevyn and Sean passed the audition and got the job, in fact Jimmy Cliff had seen the 'Shakedowns' at an all-nighter at the Whiskey-a-Go-Go in Birmingham only a few months previously. Also in the band was Verdon Allen from Hereford on keyboards, who later went on to join 'Mott the Hoople'. Kevyn and Sean moved down to London, staying in Muswell Hill. Kevyns's rasping, chopping guitar style worked well and Jimmy Cliff often used to 'toast' during the set; a forerunner of today's rap. Sean Jenkins soon got into the fashion and sported cropped hair, boots and braces in the contemporary 'rude boy' style.

Jimmy Cliff had a big following in the West Indian community and they performed regularly at venues like the Ram Jam in Brixton, the Roaring Twenties, also in London, and the Ridgeway Georgian in Handsworth. The Dungeon Club in Nottingham was another good venue where both Jimmy Cliff and Jimi Hendrix would appear on the same bill. Kevyn remembers Jimi Hendrix in the dressing room of the Dungeon playing Don Covay songs on a portable record player and then jamming afterwards. They also played at the famous 'Bag o' Nails' nightclub in London where the likes of Jimi Hendrix, Pete Townsend and Eric Clapton would turn up and cheer when Kevyn let loose on numbers like John Lee Hooker's, *'Hobo Blues'* and Jimmy Smith's *'The Cat'* during their warm up act before Jimmy Cliff came on stage. Back in Kidderminster, the band always got a great reception when they played local venues the Black Horse, the Town Hall, Frank Freeman's and the Chateau Impney at Droitwich.

In May 1967 Jimmy Cliff had a hit with *'Give and Take'* which was released on the Island label. During this month Jimmy and the 'Shakedowns' did a gig at the Black Horse. On the same bill that night were the 'Band of Joy' with Robert Plant on vocals, who were a soul outfit at the time. A few months later, the two groups bumped into each other again at the Adelphi Ballroom in West Bromwich.   Robert Plant and Kevyn Gammond got talking and Robert told Kevyn that he was reforming 'The Band of Joy' in a different direction. Roberts' enthusiasm with talk of 'Dreams of utopia' appealed to Kevyn and shortly afterwards he left Jimmy Cliff and was replaced by Mick Ralph (later of Mott the Hoople).

THE BAND OF JOY
1967 - 1968

   The line up was Robert Plant – vocals, Kevyn Gammond – guitar, Paul Lockey – bass, John Bonham – drums and Chris Brown – keyboards. Their music was experimental and part of the new counter-culture. They even had their own psychedelic light show, conjured up by local Kidderminster college student Abdul Benson. Locally they played at Frank Freeman's, the Black Horse and the Chateau Impney. In London a great gig for them was Middle Earth in Convent Garden, the home of the new 'psychedelic groups'. They also went down really well

l to r: Chris Brown, higher-
John Bonham
lower- Kevyn Gammond, Paul
Lockey, RRobert Plant
Photo: George Kristic

at the famous London 'in' club the Speakeasy. Robert Plant in particular was picking up a big reputation for his searing vocals. It was during this time that they recorded four tracks at Regent Sound Studios in London, including a powerful version of *'Hey Joe'*. The other tracks were *'Memory Lane'*, *'For What Its Worth '*(a Buffalo Springfield cover) and *'Adriatic Sea View'* which was later included in a compilation cassette *In the Forest* released by Kidderminster College, care of Kevyn Gammond. 'The Move' manager Tony Secunda had taken an interest in them, but it was never followed up.

In the summer of 1968, while gigging at the Boston Gliderdrome, Robert Plant had impressed Terry Reid who recommended him to Jimmy Page who was forming a new 'Yardbirds' at the time. Terry had been in the frame for the job himself but was more interested in forming his own group. Robert left the 'Band of Joy' and they split up. He did some work with Alexis Korner for a while but nothing was certain for Robert at this time. He went into the Golden Lion in Bushbury (Wolverhampton) one night where Walsall based 'Hobstweedle' were playing (their drummer John Trickett had been with the 'Band of Joy' for a short time when John Bonham had been with 'Way of Life' and Tim Rose). Robert joined 'Hobstweedle' for a few months. They were rehearsing in the Three Men in a Boat in Walsall when Robert received a telegram inviting him to join the 'New Yardbirds'. The band became of course 'LED ZEPPELIN'. Robert recommended John Bonham on drums who joined with him. 'Hobstweedle' keyboard player Billy Bonham (no relation) was also picked out to join Terry Reid's new group, while Kevyn Gammond formed 'Mad Dog' who later transformed into 'Bronco' with old 'Shakedown' friends Jess Roden and Johnny Pasternak.

TOMMY AND THE CRESTAS

1962 - 1971

'Tommy and the Crestas' were originally known as 'The Crestas'. Early in 1962 their singer Alfie Knott left them so they went out as a four piece: Nigel Bache, lead guitar; Dave Mansfield,rhythm guitar and vocals; Tim Wilson, bass and Nigel Turral, drums and in the summer of 1962 they played a Grand Twist Session on the King George playing fields in Franche. Shortly after this Tommy Noyes joined the band as vocalist, this was the beginning of 'Tommy and the Crestas'. Tommy was a workmate of Dave Mansfield at

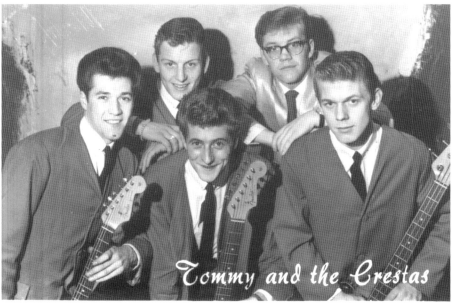

l to r: Dave Mansfield, Nigel Turrall, Nigel Bache, Tommy Noyes, Tim Wilson

Parsons Chain. Dave had heard Tommy singing all day at work and persuaded him to join the group. From now on there was no stopping them, they became one of Wyre Forest's most popular groups in the mid 1960s. They played every conceivable venue within a fifteen mile radius of Kidderminster. They did the usual support spots to 'Freddy and the Dreamers' and 'The Eagles' (from Bristol) at Kidderminster Town Hall, 'Edison Lighthouse' at Hartlebury Parish Hall and 'The Merseybeats' at Stourbridge Town Hall. They also played at Archdales club in Worcester where they supported 'Sounds Incorporated' and 'The Fortunes'. They were also active on the talent contest front ,winning a beat contest in Quarry Bank in August 1964 and coming second to 'Cliff Ward and the Cruisers' at the Locarno in Birmingham. In those years before the arrival of disco, 'Tommy and the Crestas' would knock out most of the hits of the day. The first line up change came in 1965 when Tim Wilson left and Dave Arnold from 'The Victors' took over on bass. (Many years later Tim Wilson died a tragic death when he fell off a ladder at Mullers in Cleobury). It was not until the end of 1967 that another change ocurred, when Dave Pountey

At the Locarno,
Birmingham. January
1964

joined on keyboards. Dave Arnold left in March 1968 and was replaced on

bass by Roger Mason. Another three years elapsed when in 1971 Tommy Noyes left and Chris Connelly took over on vocals. This was the end of the classic 'Tommy and the Crestas' line up. They carried on as 'The Crestas' for a bit until the vocalist changed again when Chris Connelly left and was replaced by Dave Mountain. They then moved into the cabaret circuit as 'The Association Show Band' which lasted until 1975.

It was another fifteen years before 'Tommy and the Crestas' reformed; first Dave Arnold took over on bass and then later Brian Glass. Once again Tommy Noyes left and was replaced by Peter Wynne on vocals, the band reverting to the name 'The Crestas'. Peter Wynne and Nigel Bache were regulars in the Brintons Arms in Stourport, when the subjects of groups came up. Peter told Nigel of his long career in show business, Peter had been a ballad singer in the rock n'roll era of the late fifties, early sixties and had been on the legendary Gene Vincent- Eddie Cochran tour. Peter joined 'The Crestas' and sang with them for a couple of years until he had to give up because of throat problems. Brian Glass took over on vocals while Tony Hookson joined on bass. Dave Mansfield moved from rhythm guitar to keyboards.He then left and was replaced by Rob on keyboards.

When Rob announced he was leaving to join 'Blind Lemon', 'The Crestas' decided to call it a day. Their last ever gig was at Stourport Carnival in September 1999. For longevity and the numbers of gigs played, 'Tommy and the Crestas' must take first prize; it was forty years from when Alfie Knott first came into the Birches to check out a young skiffle group, to when they finally called it a day in a marquee at Stourport Carnival.

CLIFF WARD AND THE CRUISERS
1962 - 1965

- were formed in the summer of 1962. Cliff Ward, born and brought up in Stourport, had played in a school group while at King Charles called 'The Senators''. With Cliff on vocals, the other two members of the trio were Bob Newton and Bob Spencer. They managed to get a gig at Walshes Tenants Hall in Stourport supporting another local outfit 'The Vampires'. (Ray Percy – vocals, Graham Drew and John Wainwright – guitars, and a dark haired

At the Blackhorse
l to r: Trevor Jones, Butch Bowen, Cliff Ward,
Kneeling: Graham Drew,
Rodney Simmonds.

mystery drummer from Bradford!).

After the gig, Cliff got talking to Graham and found out that he was unhappy in the group, so together they decided to form a new band. Graham knew a guitarist, Rodney Simmonds, and soon persuaded him to join them on rhythm guitar, over a cup of frothy coffee in the Coventry café. Next up was to find a bass player.

This time Graham pointed them in the direction of Trevor Jones and found him in Duffy's café in Stourport, playing the pinball machine. Trevor was told he was going to be their bass player, which was news to him. He had a six string guitar, on which Graham taught him the rudiments, until he bought himself a bass. Rodney chose the name 'Cliff Ward and the Cruisers' and rehearsals began. Only a drummer was missing. They eventually found him down at the Wharf at Holt Fleet, where Roger Bowen was drumming with a country and western outfit 'The Rebel Rousers'. He had previously drummed for 'The Zodiacs'. Rodney, Graham and Trevor spoke to Roger after the gig and talked him into joining the group, telling him about this great singer they had. So rehearsals began in earnest at the Crown in Stourport, watched over with a kindly eye by the licensees Renee and Jock Bell.

Early gigs for 'The Cruisers' included Birchen Coppice Church Hall and St Mary's Hall with 'The Cadillacs'. With Rodney's dad Fred as manager, the gigs started coming in thick and fast. Fred, a travelling carpet salesman, had the contacts and boundless enthusiasm; a downside of this in those pre-breathalyser days was Fred's fondness for the drink, the journeys home from the gigs being somewhat erratic.

Regular venues for 'The Cruisers' were the Fountain, the Black Horse, Jon and Patti's dance school in Stourport, the Golden Cross in Alcester and Sunday nights in Henley-in- Arden. Fred even got somebody from the Mecca Ballroom chain to check them out at The Fountain. They were offered a twelve-month contract which Cliff refused to sign, an early sign of his stubbornness or perhaps common sense, weighing up all the factors. In January 1963, they won through to the finals of the Midland Band of the Year contest, and in March at the Locarno Ballroom in Birmingham, they actually won the event doing *La Bamba*. The group, but not Cliff, dressed up in Mexican gear, Tim Jackson deputising for Roger Bowen on drums. (Roger had injured himself playing football). This was quite an achievement, although nothing really came of it, so it was back to the regular one -nighters.

By now Cliff was making some tentative attempts at song- writing, he wanted to steer away from the standard rock and pop of the day. A clash with Fred Simmonds was inevitable, Fred was a hard worker but lacked vision and was very domineering, coming on like Larry Parnes, trying to stop Pat, Cliff Ward's wife, from coming along to gigs. Fred realised his time was up and left. He was replaced by Finlay Tinker as manager.

Rehearsals were often tense affairs. Cliff had a perfect ear and Trevor recalls him being a stickler for perfection. Tension had been building up between Cliff and Rodney Simmonds for some time, which came to a head with a rather unpleasant fight. A few days later Rodney left the band.

Finlay placed an ad in the local press and was contacted by Terry Clarke. Terry, whose family ran a successful grocery business in Kidderminster, was playing with 'Alfie Knott and the AK's' at the time, (formerly known as 'The Sunsetters'). Cliff and Terry hit it off immediately, so Terry became Rodney's replacement as rhythm guitarist. Finlay eventually tired of being a pop group manager and his place was taken by Terry Clarke's brother Phil, who secured them a working holiday playing the Welsh coastal resorts, a popular gig for semi-pro groups during the 1960s. This signalled the departure of the original member of 'The Cruisers', Roger Bowen. Roger loved drumming in the band, the socialising, meeting girls, it was all great fun, but he had no pretensions to turning professional. In any case he was dedicated to the family butcher's business in Stourport.

in action at the Tower Ballroom, Edgbaston.

So in came Ken Wright. Ken had played drums in the fading days of the local dance bands and also trad jazz with Alan Worrells 'Apex Jazz Band', so drumming for a pop group was no problem. The tour of Wales went ahead. The De Valence Ballroom Tenby, The Fountain Café, Milford Haven, and The Tower Ballroom, Swansea. Upon their return they had a support spot on the newly started Thursday night Big Beat Sessions at Kidderminster Town Hall, supporting ex-boxer Mike Preston.

As the gigs and rehearsals continued, more obscure American numbers with vocal harmonies were replacing the rock 'n roll standards. Learning these numbers with Cliff in charge was a form of pure torture, but they carried on although from time to time Cliff would walk off-stage in the middle of a set in a fit of pique. I actually witnessed this myself one night standing in the audience in the Black Horse. Anyway, they re-entered the band of the year contest at the Locarno in January 1964, coming joint first in the semi-finals with the 'Plainsmen', beating off competition from local rivals 'Tommy and the Cresta's'. The night was somewhat spoilt by a mike, guitar and amp being stolen from the dressing room. In the finals, they played 'Big Dee Irwin's *Swingin' on a Star*' with Trevor and Graham dressed in mule's head masks. This time they were unplaced – 'The Plainsmen' won, and irony of ironies 'The Simonals' from Kidderminster came third, managed by guitarist Ian Simmond's dad, Fred. Exit one more manager who, as usual, always gets the blame; Phillip Clarke didn't mind, he was off to Australia anyway. In stepped manager number four, Roger Rowe, son of Mr Rowe of Rowe Carpets. Regular gigs at the Park Attwood in Trimpley followed, Roger's family home bordered the hotel. Roger worked hard for the band and followed them to all their gigs before having to give up and pay attention to the serious business of making carpets for the family firm. So in stepped management number five, Park Attwood promoters Peter Phillips and Nigel Reece. They supervised another summer season at Tenby, the band having to sleep on the stage of the De Valence Ballroom on the first night, due to a mix up in booking rooms. There was another dance hall close by where Birmingham 'Mike Sheridan and the Nightriders' were resident. Sometimes the bands used to get together and swapped venues without telling anybody; all good fun.

On their return home, the usual gigs followed including the Nautical William. It was there that Cliff's refusal to ever play a 'Beatles' number got them into a tight spot. As the audience kept asking for them to do some 'Beatles' songs, Cliff of course turned them down, so the chairs began to fly, mostly directed towards the stage. They managed to escape relatively unscathed but never played the Nautical William again ! They had an interesting gig supporting legendary rock 'n'roll stars Little Richard and Gene Vincent at Wolverhampton Civic. 'The Cruisers' were on in the afternoon and Peter Phillips recalls never having seen Cliff so nervous, and, to cap it all, one of the amps was playing up. However he somehow managed to get through the gig. Practise sessions continued as normal at the Crown, although on one unfortunate occasion with Ken Wright's van doors unlocked, some locals took the opportunity to steal the group's PA system, but they managed to get themselves re-equipped and the usual gigs continued.

Cliff was also experimenting with some of his own songs on tape, aided by local tape enthusiast Leon Tipler. Cliff even got together with Rodney Simmonds to help him out on acoustic guitar with some songs he'd written. It was at these sessions that Leon instigated some comedy tapes when local beauty Teresa Oakley joined with the others to record 'The Gloria Bosom Show'. More serious recordings took place at the Hollick and Taylor studios in Birmingham. They recorded four numbers, two covers and a Cliff and Graham composition *'Ooh-wee-Baby'* and Cliffs own song *'Rachel'*. The demos were sent off and they actually got a positive reply from Columbia who booked them into the famous Abbey Road Studios on February 1st 1965. They recorded one of Holland-Dozier-Holland's weaker songs *'Candy To Me'*, backing vocals supplied by two local girls, Peter Phillip's sister Carol and of course Teresa Oakley. Columbia were satisfied with the record and a release date was set for May. They had one problem; they had to change their name to avoid confusion with Dave Berry and the Cruisers. They became known as:

MARTIN RAYNOR AND THE SECRETS
1965 - 1967

To promote the record they went down to London for a photo session and to record the song for a Radio Luxembourg transmission at a later date. On its release on Friday May 7th, it knocked 'The Beatles' *'Ticket to Ride'* off the number one spot – in Kidderminster of course – staying there for two weeks; in the rest of the country it disappeared without trace. Having gone professional the band signed up with the local Mercian Agency, and a tour was arranged to play US bases in France, a traditional way for a group to toughen up and get more professional before hopefully hitting the big time in the UK.

Their first stop was a base just outside Fontainebleau, not a great gig really, the servicemen were expecting a girl singer and they were also waiting to go to Vietnam. Anyway they saw it through, although Cliff in particular was very homesick, wandering through the woods near Fontainebleau, or the nearby war graves. It was during this period that he may well have had the idea of a song, the wonderful *'Home Thoughts From Abroad'*. After Fontainebleau, they moved on to St Dizier, a more pleasant

COLUMBIA
RECORDS

l to r: Graham Drew, Trevor Jones, Terry Clarke, Ken Wright, Cliff Ward, Carol Phillips, Teresa Oakley.

booking. They stayed in an old hotel, a great improvement to living on the base. They had been there about two weeks when a huge electric storm broke out during their set. Terry refused to play, stating it was too dangerous especially with the poor wiring. "Play or you're fired" was the ultimatum. These were the words the band were waiting for. They packed the gear up and headed straight for the ferry and home, they'd all had enough. This soujorn in France hadn't been a complete waste of time, as the germs of songs had been awakened in Cliff, and, of more immediate use, Terry Clarke had recorded a load of American soul records played to them by one of the friendlier GIs. They had a whole set's worth of material to rehearse when they got home, and rehearse they did, intensively, at the Mare and Colt. For Graham and Trevor a career as a professional musician was not to be and they both handed in their notice, paradoxically Trevor needed a regular wage to pay for his equipment. Kevyn Gammond joined temporarily on lead after the split up of 'The Shakedowns', a rather bizarre situation, as Kevyn and the Secrets were poles apart musically. Kevyn used to play '*T-Bone Shuffle*' by T-Bone Walker, and persuaded Cliff to sing a couple of Paul Butterfield songs. Paul Turner, ex 'Shades 5', took over on bass also on a temporary basis, and keyboard player David Floyd also made a brief appearance. Before Trevor and Graham left a second single had been recorded for Columbia, entitled '*Imagination*' – it was never released. In April 1966, Ken Wright received a letter from Jimmy Page who was working for Immediate at the time, saying he liked a song he had heard on a demo called '*Infatuation*'. The group shot down to London straight away, to the

IBC studios, where Bill Wyman sat in with Jimmy Page and legendary record producer Glyn Johns. The recording sessions went well, but in spite of Jimmy Page's enthusiasm the recordings were never released, Jimmy Page joined the 'Yardbirds' in June 1966. A version of the *'Gloria Bosom Song'* was later released by 'The Sundowners', for which Cliff received the princely sum of £15.

By June 1966 Kevyn Gammond had joined another Cliff, this time it was Jamaican singer Jimmy Cliff, and Paul Turner had also left. Terry Clarke was promoted from rhythm to lead and Malcolm Russell from Smethwick joined on bass. This line up didn't last too long when Terry Clarke announced he was off to Australia to join his brother Phil. Panic station. There was a London booking at the Flamingo and another tour arranged, and record companies were still showing an interest, Malcolm Russell suggested a friend of his, Fred Nash to take over on lead. Fred joined and turned out to be a very good guitarist. This was the last line up that Cliff sang with in a group format.

Somehow or other the Jimmy Page tapes had found their way to an independent record producer, Cornishman Eddie Trevett. He met up with the band in Torquay while they were on a tour of the southwest, and secured a one off publishing deal with Terry Oates and a singles contract with CBS. Eddie Trevett produced the single *'I Suppose'*, a Cliff Ward composition, with *'Such A Pity'* on the B side. This record, Cliff's second release went out on December 2nd 1966, credited to 'The Secrets', Cliff having got rid of his alter-ego Martin Raynor. Another tour of South Wales followed, but a trip to London from there for a publicity shot ended abruptly when Ken Wright crashed the van on a hairpin bend, not a brilliant end to a promising but frustrating year.

A further two singles were released by CBS in 1967. First was *'Infatuation'* with *'She's Dangerous'* on the B-side. Then later on *'I Intend To Please'* was released on June 23rd with *'I Think I Need The Cash'* on the B-side. None of these singles had any success. In February the band parted company with the Mercian Agency and the number of gigs dropped considerably, although Eddie Trevett also ran an agency and got them gigs at Tiles in London's Oxford Street and the Purple Fez in Plymouth. With the lack of gigs the group had virtually become defunct. Ken Wright in fact had been depping at the Beachcomber in Nottingham for 'Jimmy Cliff and the Shakedowns' thanks to Kevyn Gammond. They were on the point of splitting up when news came through that they had passed an audition for Radio One to be recorded at the BBC's Paris studios in London's Regent Street. So, off they went back down to London again, this time augmented by Worcester keyboard player Tony Scriven. Cliff as usual was extremely tense. Dave Cash fronted the show, they followed Cat Stevens who sang 'Matthew And Son'. Their first number was their latest single 'I Intend To Please', for their second they did a song called 'Two People', a catchy commercial numbe. Nobody knows where it came from although Cliff insisted he wrote it himself. The show was called 'Monday, Monday' and went out on the 28th August, 1967 – it disappeared totally into the ether. This was the end of the group scene for Cliff, the band split up. Cliff was disillusioned by the music business and more to the point he was, as usual, extremely short of cash, with a young family to bring up. So with the demand for teachers and Cliff's love of language and books, he enrolled at the Worcester Teaching Training Centre in September 1967. Thus ended the first chapter in Cliff Ward's musical career; not stopped, just temporarily on hold.

CLIFF WARD DISCOGRAPHY 1965/1967
SINGLES

Candy To Me/ You're A Wonderful One	Columbia May 1965
I Suppose/Such A Pity	CBS December 1966
Infatuation/She's Dangerous	CBS March 1967
I Intend To Please/I Think I Need The Cash	CBS June 1967

THE WARD FIVE
1963 - 1964

...were formerly known as 'The Rolling Stones'. They changed their name in the summer of 1963 because of the popularity of another group from London with the same name.

They had recently bought an old ambulance from Smethwick Hospital to use as a group van, and changed their name to 'The Ward Five'. Ray Harris had just taken over the vocals from Bob Bullen, the others were: Robert Smith, lead guitar; Martin Smith, rhythm; Ian Hardiman, bass; and Ron Griffiths, drums. They did plenty of work for promoter Norman Dickens at Kidderminster and Stourbridge Town Halls supporting 'The Hollies', 'Bern Elliot and the Fenmen', 'Dave Berry and the Cruisers', 'Gene Vincent and the Outlaws', 'Johnny Kidd and the Pirates', 'Unit 4+2,' 'Manfred Mann' and 'The Small Faces'.

l to r: Martin Smith, Robert Smith, Ian Hardiman, Ron Griffiths, on roof Ray Harris

In the summer of 1964 they won a beat contest at Tomkinson's Club, The Oaklands, beating 'The Simonals' into second place. In the autumn of 1964 the Smith brothers moved with their families to North Wales, this split the band up. Ray Harris and Ian Hardiman went on to join 'The Zodiacs'.

THE WHIRLWINDS
1963 - 1964

'The Whirlwinds' were formed by three King Charles Grammar School boys: Ivan Vaux, Lofty Saunders and Ian 'Inky' Watts, keyboards, bass and lead guitar respectively, with Fred Randall on drums and Bruce 'Maverick' Oakes' on rhythm completing the line up.

Their material was mainly instrumentals by bands like 'The Tornados' and 'The Shadows'. Later on a few 'Beatles' and 'Stones' numbers were added with Ian 'Inky' Watts on vocals. Their stage gear at this time consisted of glittery jackets in either silver or blue.

When they had their first gig at Clows Top, the group had to travel there on the bus with their equipment. All the instruments had to go through one Watkins Dominator amp. Later on they acquired their own transport and some Vox AC30s. Other early venues for them were Wribbenhall Parish Rooms, The Labour Club, The Fountain and Kidderminster Town Hall. They split up early in 1964. Bruce Oakes and Ian Watts went on to join 'The Crawling Kingsnakes'.

PEOPLE AND EVENTS

1963-1967

The beat scene really exploded during this period. Just about everybody was in a group, playing in youth clubs, pubs, carnivals, anywhere in fact you could squeeze a group and an audience. The country's top groups appeared at Kidderminster Town Hall. As usual all this activity was chronicled by the Shuttle. There was also ominous indicators of the 'redevelopment' of the town centre.

1963

Monday 14th January
> 'Cliff Ward and the Cruisers' win first heat of a beat contest at The Locarno in Birmingham, which guaranteed them a place in the March finals.

Sunday 17th March
> 'Summer Holiday' starring Cliff Richard began a 7-day run at the Central. Stan Webb's 'Strangers Incorporated' played live before the film was shown.

Monday 1st April
> 'Billy Liar' was on at the 'Playhouse Theatre'. While the controversial film 'Lolita' appeared at 'The Central' with James Mason, Peter Sellers, Shelley Winters and Sue Lyon.

Thursday 25th April
> The Chris Barber Jazz Band' appeared at Kidderminster Town Hall, with OtilliePatterson on vocals.

Thursday 9th May

For three nights, crooner Ronnie Carroll appeared at The Playhouse along with the 'Hedley Ward Trio'. Tickets were free and the whole show was sponsored by Kensistas Cigarettes!

Monday 20th May

For six days at The Central cinema was 'Whatever Happened to Baby Jane?' Starring Bette Davies and Joan Crawford.

Friday 24th May

An article appeared in the Shuttle about a new £2,000 Cinebox which had been installed into the Flamingo Café in Mill Street. It had a screen, which actually showed a film of the artists singing the song that was playing, in full colour. Quite an innovation for those days, but not a commercial success.

Friday 31st May

Dance hall hooligans got a severe warning from local magistrates after a mass brawl at a dance at Hartlebury Parish Hall. The scene was described like something out of the Wild West.

Friday 12th July

'Big Dave and The Hangmen' won a talent contest at St. Johns Parish Hall.

Saturday 13th July

'Mr Moon River', Danny Williams, crowned the carnival Queen at Birchen Coppice Carnival. There was a dance in the evening at St. Peters Church Hall, music provided by 'The Whirlwinds'.

Saturday 27th July

There was a Civic Farewell to the Lion Hotel at the top of the High Street. This much loved hostelry had been a coaching inn built in 1790, originally called the White Lion. In 1906 Stanley Baldwin stood on its balcony and addressed his supporters after losing at a parliamentary election. The Lion was to be demolished to make way for a Woolworth's store, along with its next-door neighbour The Wheatsheaf pub. This was an act of gross vandalism unfortunately repeated many times in the ensuing years.

Thursday 15th August

The famous Big Beat sessions started at Kidderminster Town Hall with 'Mike Berry and The Innocents'. With 'The Outlaws', Mike Berry had two hits in 1963: *'Don't You Think Its Time?'* and the classic *'Tribute To Buddy Holly'*. The following weeks featured appearances by 'Brian Poole and the Tremoloes' and 'The Searchers'.

Friday 16th August

The landlord of the Green Man, Mr Peter Shepley-Taylor, started live music sessions, with a band from Blackheath called 'The Blizzards'. Was this the start of pub rock?

Friday 30th August

Twenty-year old Tommy Noyes, singer with 'The Crestas' won the Grundig Pop Vocalist's competition at Butlins holiday camp, Pwllheli, this week.

Tommy Noyes at Pwllheli
August 1963

Saturday 7th September

Pop singer Mike Preston crowned Stourport Carnival Queen, Trudi Turner. In the evening he played Kidderminster Town Hall, supported by 'Cliff Ward and The Cruisers'. On the same day ' The Simonals' won the Stourport Carnival Beat Competition.

Friday 13th September

'Acker Bilk with his Paramount Jazz Band' appeared at Kidderminster Town Hall. A new floor had just been laid.

Friday 1st November

A Big Beat all-nighter was arranged at the Florence with 'Cliff Ward and The Cruisers', 'Mark Stuart and the Crestas', 'Johnny Neal and the Starliners' and 'The Clippers'. 'The Swinging Blue Jeans' were booked to headline the show but didn't turn up.

Friday 22nd November

Mr Peter Shepley–Taylor, licensee of the Green Man was refused permission for an alcohol license for Kidderminster Baths Ballroom, when 'The Blizzards' would be playing, as there would be too many teenagers there.

Monday 2nd December

The film 'Tom Jones' was on at the Central for six days, starring Albert Finney and Susanna York.

1964

Friday 3rd January

A full page announcement was taken out in the Shuttle stating that the Playhouse would close in May 1964 unless Rate Relief was granted and blaming the Kidderminster public in general, the Borough Council, the Arts Council and the Operatic Societies for lack of support, both financially and lack of attending at the Playhouse.

Friday 17th January

"Jazz at the Boat Club - will it survive?" were the headlines in the entertainment pages of the Shuttle. The article stated that jazz sessions at the Crown in Stourport, the Manor in Bewdley and Kidderminster Town Hall have all stopped because of lack of support, and that jazz at the Stourport Boat Club was also in danger of finishing. This prediction came true a week later when it was announced that jazz at the Boat Club was finished due to poor attendance, and that Rhythm and Blues group 'Shades Five' would take over on Saturday nights.

Friday 24th January

Things were going well for 'Cliff Ward and the Cruisers'. Their manager, Roger Rowe, had just announced that the group now had their own fan club, the first in the area, the secretary would be Marion Dredge from Habberley estate.

Saturday 1st February

Two of the 'Swinging Blue Jeans', Ralph Ellis and Norman Kuhlke went two hundred feet down a mineshaft at Hunt House Colliery, Clows Top. They said afterwards "its more like dig that crazy coal, than dig that crazy beat!" 'The Swinging Blue Jeans' were number two in the charts with the '*Hippy, Hippy Shake*', and had just appeared at Kidderminster Town Hall on Thursday night.

Friday 7th February

Local teenage group 'The Simonals' won a talent competition at Malvern Winter Gardens, beating nine other contestants; the average age of the band was fifteen. In the same issue of the Shuttle, Brian Wilson of Startime Promotions announced that there would be 'Twist and Shake' sessions at Bleak House Country Club in Stourport. First group would be 'The Four Aces' from Ludlow, followed next week by popular group 'Earl Grant and the Zodiacs'.

Friday 21st February

A bar extension was refused to the licensee who ran the bar at Hartlebury Parish Hall. The police objected on the grounds that open warfare had occurred there recently at a local dance, when twenty youths were fighting after they got in for late drinks. A similar situation had occurred at the Fountain on January 24th when gangs of brawling youths had ruined a young Liberal dance. On the bill that night were 'The Strangers' and 'The Whirlwinds'.

Thursday 5th March

Huge queues formed at Kidderminster Town Hall, past Brintons offices and into Corporation Street. They had all come to see 'Freddy and the Dreamers'.

Friday 6th March

It was announced that Peter Phillips and Nigel Reece were starting to promote groups at the Park Attwood.

Sunday 6th March

Blue Beat sessions started at Frank Freeman's every Sunday.

Monday 9th March

The film 'The Servant', screenplay by Harold Pinter was on at the ABC Cinema (formerly The Central). It starred Dirk Bogarde, Sarah Miles and James Fox.

Thursday 26th March

'The Rolling Stones' appeared at Kidderminster Town Hall. Huge queues formed in the early afternoon. The promoter apologised for having to charge 8/6d (42 1/2p), saying that "these fabulous artists charge fantastic fees".

Saturday 11th April

After their appearance at The Central for ABC minors, local r'n'b band 'Shades Five' headed to London for a recording session.

Monday 1st June

Billy Smart's Circus came to town for five days; they pitched down at a site on the Stourport Road.

Sometime between the 19th and the 21st of June.

The National Provincial bank in the High Street was robbed of £24,000; the safe was blown open with gelignite. The robbers had time to brew up a pot of tea while they were there.

Saturday 20th June

Johnny Kidd from' Johnny Kidd and the Pirates' crowned sixteen-year-old Pat Robinson as carnival Queen at the Birchen Coppice Carnival.

Saturday 18th July

Fifteen year old 'pop singer' Shirley Moncrief was crowned Wolverley Carnival Queen, music provided on a stage outside the Queens Head by the 'Big C's' beat group.

Monday 3rd August

Teenage band 'The Simonals' came second in a beat contest at the Far Forest Show. 'Maureen and the Stringbeats' from Stourport came third.

Saturday 22nd August

Fourteen year old Lorraine Tongue from Bewdley won a talent contest at the ABC Cinema backed by her group 'The Invaders'.

Sunday 23rd August

'The Beatles' appeared for a week at the ABC in 'A Hard Days Night', directed by Dick Lester. The film got a good review in the local press.

Saturday 29th August

'Tommy and the Crestas' won a beat competition in Quarry Bank against eight other groups. 'The Scorpions' from Kinver came second.

Saturday 5th September

'The Count' is counted out at fifteen seconds, watched by astonished customers at 'The Peacock Inn'. Bert Taylor, drank a yard of ale (2 pints) in fifteen seconds. He had already drunk twelve pints of mild. He said this was only one second slower than the time recorded by the British Champion Yard of Ale drinker.

Saturday 14th November

Kidderminster Harriers lost 4-1 to Hull City at Aggborough in the first round of the F.A cup. 6,610 fans attended the match.

Saturday 12th December

'The Zombies' played at Kidderminster Bath's Ballroom, support was 'The Stringbeat's' and 'R' n'B Incorporated'.

1965

Monday 3rd Jan

The classic James Bond film 'Goldfinger' appeared at the ABC Cinema for seven days, starring Sean Connery and Honor Blackman. At the same time Larry Grayson appeared at the Playhouse as 'Widow Twanky' in the pantomime 'Aladdin'. Also this week trad jazz started up again at The George in Bewdley.

Thursday 14th Jan

At the ABC for three days was the classic 60s film 'Saturday Night Sunday Morning'. starring Albert Finney and Shirley Ann Field.

Friday 19th Feb

Eden Kane appeared at the Town Hall with support band 'The Nomads'. Jazz was to start up again at the Fountain on Monday January 21st.

Friday 26th February

Another old Kidderminster pub bites the dust. The Cross Keys in Worcester Street was demolished to make way for a new £150,000 Tesco store.

Monday 8th March

There was a double bill this week at the ABC with 'Lord of the Flies' for the first three days, followed for the next three by another James Bond classic 'Dr No' with Sean Connery and Ursula Andress.

Friday 23rd April

It was announced that 'Cliff Ward and the Cruisers' would change their name to 'Martin Raynor and the Secrets' to coincide with their first single to be released on May 7th, entitled *'Candy To Me'*. The name change was due to avoid confusion with 'Dave Berry and the Cruisers'.

Thursday 22nd April

Tom Jones made a guest appearance at the Worcester Cross Youth Club to talk to handicapped youngsters there. After having dinner at Charles Talbot 's house Tom Jones went to do an evening performance at the Town Hall.

Wednesday 12th May 1

Was the official opening of the 'Riverboat Inn', one of the new style Bernie Inn restaurants. This was on the premises of the Florence ballroom. With its different themed restaurants it proved an instant success.

Friday 14th May

'Candy To Me' by 'Martin Raynor and the Secrets' reached number one in the local top ten, knocking 'The Beatles' – *'Ticket To Ride'* off the number one spot.

Between Friday 21st and 28th May

The new Mayor, 33 yr old young Charles Talbot, launched a youth fund to improve facilities for the town's teenagers and to provide a central youth centre for the whole town.

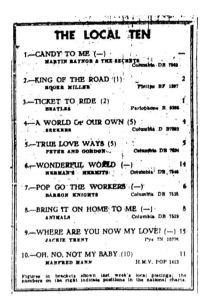

THE LOCAL TEN

1.—CANDY TO ME (—)   —
         MARTIN RAYNOR & THE SECRETS
                              Columbia DB 7542

2.—KING OF THE ROAD (1)   2
         ROGER MILLER   Philips BF 1397

3.—TICKET TO RIDE (2)   1
         BEATLES   Parlophone R 5265

4.—A WORLD OF OUR OWN (5)   4
         SEEKERS   Columbia D B7382

5.—TRUE LOVE WAYS (5)   5
         PETER AND GORDON   Columbia DB 7524

6.—WONDERFUL WORLD (—)   14
         HERMAN'S HERMITS   Columbia DB 7546

7.—POP GO THE WORKERS (—)   6
         BARRON KNIGHTS   Columbia DB 7525

8.—BRING IT ON HOME TO ME (—)   8
         ANIMALS   Columbia DB 7539

9.—WHERE ARE YOU NOW MY LOVE? (—) 15
         JACKIE TRENT   Pye 7N 15776

10.—OH, NO, NOT MY BABY (10)   11
         MANFRED MANN   H.M.V. POP 1413

Figures in brackets shown last week's local placings; the numbers on the right indicate positions in the national charts.

'*Candy To Me*' reaches number one in the local top ten

Friday 2nd July

A group of railway enthusiasts met to discuss plans to run the old Severn Valley line. This turned out in time to be the hugely successful Severn Valley Railway, one of the town's real success stories.

Monday 25th July

For six days at the ABC, 'Lawrence of Arabia' with Peter O'Toole, Jack Hawkins, Anthony Quinn and Alex Guinness.

Friday 16th July

"Theatre Doomed" were the headlines. The Playhouse, after years of financial problems, was finally given the death sentence; it was to be demolished to make way for the ring road.

Wednesday 4th August

Work began on the £400,000 inner ring road, a black day for Kidderminster. This act of wanton destruction ripped out the heart of the old part of town.

Thursday 19th August

Folk/Pop singer Donovan who appeared at the Town Hall that night was interviewed by Shuttle reporter Richard Brooks. Donovan said that his fans "Don't scream much for me anymore, they have grown to accept me". This seemed to belie the fact as a large gang of teenage girls at the front screamed and groped at Donovan, throughout his acoustic set. (His support band and PA system hadn't turned up). Yobbish cries of ' Dylan' from the boys at the back of the hall didn't help either. Richard Brooks found Donovan a sincere and genuine person.

Sunday 29th August

'The Beatles' second film 'Help' was on at the ABC for seven days.

Friday 10th September

'Nashville Teens' drummer twenty-year-old Barrie Jenkins appeared in court at Kidderminster to answer charges of firearm possession at the Town Hall on August 12th . On the same night Irish folk singer Dominic Behan, brother of the famous poet Brendan Behan, appeared at Stourport Folk Club Festival as a last minute replacement for Cyril Tawney. Also on the bill that night was Fred Raybould from Stourport, and Dave Cartwright from Stourbridge who performed a polished and confident set. The evening was a great success, 270 paying guests turned up.

Friday 17th September

An article appeared in the Shuttle about a hundred-year- old savings bank and almshouses with associations dating back to the seventeenth century, that were demolished the previous week to make way for the ring road.

Wednesday 29th September

The second phase of the £620,000 Kidderminster College at Aggborough was officially opened.

The year ended with a perennial problem; there were severe floods in Bewdley and Stourport with the River Severn fifteen feet above its normal level.

1966

Friday 4th January

"Factories Reprieved, Playhouse Doomed" were the Shuttle headlines. The final ring road route had been virtually settled. The Playhouse was to be demolished along with two Georgian hotels, The Worcester Cross, and the Black Horse.

Monday 31st January

'*Darling*' was at the ABC Cinema for six days, starring Julie Christie, Dirk Bogarde and Laurence Harvey.

Friday 4th February

Lloyds Bank moved to new premises at 19 Comberton Hill. This branch, which was my regular bank, was closed down in 1995; obviously they must have been short of money.

Friday 11th February

The Shuttle reported that Dudley Street and Hall Street, both which of which ran from the Horsefair to Church Street, were being knocked down to make way for the new ring road.

Friday 18th March

The Beat Scene column reported the break up of 'The Shakedown Sound' with Jess Roden joining 'The Alan Bown Set', Sean Jenkins joining Welsh group 'Eyes of Blue', Kevin Gammond taking the place of Graham Drew in the 'Secrets', while Johnny Pasternak disappeared somewhere in Birmingham. The Beat Scene was to be a regular feature in the Shuttle for a number of years. Its two writers, Richard Matthews and Malcolm Nicholl, provided a fascinating insight into the music scene of that very exciting time.

Friday 25th March

It was reported in the Beat Scene column that the 'Carlton Orchestra' had finally ended their residency at the Black Horse, after almost twenty years. The Black Horse was now to become a venue for top

Midlands groups, with the Mercian Agency responsible for bookings. 'Tommy and the Crestas' opened the venue on Friday March 18th, with 'The Huskies' to appear on the 25th. Future acts were to include 'The Suede's' from Worcester and 'Raynor's Secrets'.

Friday 1st April

The Beat Scene column featured an article on 'The Suede's' from Worcester, also that 'Tommy and The Crestas' were appearing at Kinlet Hall as part of the Horse Trials Ball. Ken Wright from 'Raynor's Secrets' reported Jimmy Page and Bill Wyman present at their latest London recording session. Finally Sean Jenkins made a swift return from Swansea to Kidderminster; apparently 'Eyes of Blue' didn't appeal.

Friday 8th April

'The Beat Scene' column reported that Robert Plant's group 'Listen' would be appearing at Frank Freeman's on Easter Sunday. It was also reported that Atwood's department store was losing its Regency Façade, another act of vandalism committed in the name of progress in Kidderminster Town Centre. How did they get away with it?

Friday 22nd April

'The Beat Scene' column featured an article declaring that there were 20 'beat dances' within a ten mile area from Kidderminster during the week, twelve of them were on Friday and Saturday nights. Good reports about 'The Indigo Set's' appearance at the Black Horse, particularly Colin Youngjohn's strong vocals.

Friday 29th April

'The Beat Scene' column reported that the promoters of the Park Attwood, Nigel Reece and Peter Phillips, had spread their wings to Droitwich where they were starting ' The Grotto Club' in the Imp Bar at the Chateau. One of the first groups to appear there was Mike Sheridan's 'Nightriders' from Birmingham.

Friday 6th May

Shuttle reports Richard Matthews visited the newly opened 'Mister Casual' boutique at the end of Worcester Street, where he tried on all the latest mod gear. Run by Bob Tansley and Paul Turner. 'Mister Casual' was the first shop in Kidderminster to specialise in the very latest mod fashion. The Beat Scene reported that the beat group sessions at the Black Horse were proving a great success with full houses almost every night.

THE INDIGO SET
outside Mr. Casual.

Friday 24th June

'The Beat Scene' featured an article on Worcester band 'Deep Feelin', formerly known as 'The Hellions'. It was reported that 'Deep Feelin' vocalist Jim Capaldi went ghost hunting at Witley Court with Steve Winwood and Bob Dylan. I have no confirmation of this interesting story. It was also reported that Terry Clark had taken over lead guitar with 'Raynors Secrets', while Malcolm Russell from Smethwick took over on bass. With Ken Wright on drums and Cliff on vocals the band were now a four- piece.

Monday 27th June

At the ABC Cinema for six days was classic 60s film '*Alfie*' starring Michael Caine.

Friday 8th July

It was reported that local groups had seaside bookings that summer. 'Martin Raynor and the Secrets' were to play Torquay, Bognor Regis, Aberystwyth, Tenby, Newquay and Prestatyn, while the 'Apper-Clarse' were to visit Ramsgate, Margate and Brighton, all booked through the Mercian Agency.

Wednesday 20th July

The newly formed 'Reflections' played at Stourport Civic. The line up was: Dave England – vocals, Graham Drew – lead guitar, Trevor Jones – bass, Rodney Simmonds – rhythm, and Alan Millward – drums.

Friday 29th July

A headline article appeared in the Shuttle "Shoplifting the thing to do". This was about eighteen local girls aged between thirteen and sixteen from the areas top schools, all daughters of professional people, who had been accused of stealing teenage essentials such as records, make up, clothes, perfume and transistor radios. It was reported that shoplifting was a form of initiation into a 'twisted café society'. They were all fined £5 on each charge.

Friday 12th August

An article on the front page of the Shuttle reported that Jess Roden with his band 'The Alan Bown Set' were heading for the charts with their version of Edwin Starr's *'Headline News'*. They had played on the famous TV music show 'Ready Steady Go' and were soon to go on tour with 'The Merseys' and 'The Who'.

Friday 19th August

An article in the Shuttle said that local drummer Rob Elcock (formerly with 'The Simonals', 'Sounds of Blue' and 'The Montanas') was touring Germany and Holland for a second time after a very successful first tour with Midlands group 'The Rishells'.

Friday 26th August

The Beat Scene reported Al Attwood rhythm guitar with 'The Indigo Set', breaking his arm and doing vocals only. The group had seaside bookings at Newquay and Aberystwyth.

Friday 2nd September

It was reported that Terry Clarke was playing his last gig for 'The Secrets' at the Black Horse. He was going to Australia to help his brother out in his nightclub in Newcastle.

Friday 16th September

'The Indigo Set' and 'Deep Feeling' appeared at Stourport Civic. 'Deep Feeling' had just released a record on Polydor entitled *'Pretty*

Flowers'. It was also reported that the Town Hall sessions would start again on Thursday, September 22nd with 'The Moody Blues'!

Friday 23rd September

'The Beat Scene' reported changes in the Kidderminster group scene. 'The Secrets' announced that twenty-year-old Fred Nash from Smethwick had taken over Terry Clarke lead guitar spot. 'Apper Clarse' bass player Dave Towers was replaced by Frank Dudley from Stourbridge. Also Al Atwood, rhythm guitarist with 'The Indigo Set,' had left for personal reasons. Meanwhile from Paris came news that Kevyn Gammond and Sean Jenkins were getting rave reviews as part of Jimmy Cliff's backing group 'The Shakedown Sound'. Finally there was news of Leon Tipler, Kidderminster tape and electronic wizard, had joined the pirate radio ship 'Radio 270' as a DJ. Leon reported having a swinging time in the North Sea.

Friday 30th September

Malcolm Nicholl of the Beat Scene reported that big names would now be appearing at Stourport Civic Centre as well as the Town Hall, courtesy of the Mercian Agency. Acts such as the 'Moody Blues', the 'Fortunes' and Spencer Davis were among the names that would be appearing. This would make the Kidderminster area the best live music town in the Midlands for its size, putting on more name acts than towns three or four times its size. Malcolm stated that locally there were a dozen venues putting on beat groups. Also reports coming from the Marquee in London that 'The Alan Bown Set' recorded a live set there. They will be on one side of the LP with 'Jimmy James and the Vagabonds' on the other.

There were also reported exciting developments on the local jazz scene with the club at the Briars putting on top class bands. The previous Monday, the Chris Barber Jazz Band appeared there. Apart from a traditional set, Chris Barber introduced a young black singer Kenneth Washington, together with a young guitarist, giving the band a very contemporary sound. The following Monday at the Briars a legendary figure of New Orleans jazz appeared there. Sixty-six year old clarinet player, George Lewis, showed extreme talent and turned in an energetic performance, accompanied by the Kid Martin band.

An article appeared in the Shuttle describing the sad rundown state of a picturesque little square of Church Street called Arch Hill Square. The properties were in a poor state of repair, the local council said it would consider renovating them if they could get financial help from central government , otherwise they would have to be demolished as part of the new town centre redevelopment. One of the residents Mrs. Hilda Munn had had enough, after waiting years to see what the council would do and hoped that some action would be taken soon, and who could blame her. I think you can guess what happened to this "Picturesque Island".

In the same issue there was another headline 'Beat Sessions upset Residents'. One of the residents complained about the noise coming from Stourport Civic Centre saying, "We might as well just be in Africa", complaining about the thumping of drums and other 'weird sounds' coming from the Civic Centre when beat dances were held there. This was an ongoing problem through the years. Stourport Civic Centre, an ideal venue for beat music should really have been built in Kidderminster town centre.

Tuesday 18th October

Town Clerk, Mr John Evans said that last year's economic crisis very nearly prevented the start of the inner ring road, it could have even set the starting date 'out of sight'; now that would have been a shame.

Wednesday 19th October

The Harriers lost 4 -2 to Hereford in an F.A cup replay at Aggborough, despite being 2 - 0 up for a time. A five thousand strong crowd turned up with hopes of a trip to Peterborough in the next round.

Thursday 1st December

'Herbie Goins and the Nightimers' played Kidderminster Town Hall on this night. They got a great review by Malcolm Nicholl. In spite of a half-full hall they eventually got the crowd going with the help of mini-skirted Candy, one of the Ready Steady Go dancers. Also in the band that night was the famous conga player 'Speedy' whose was formerly with Georgie Fame. This was the last of the famous Big Beat Sessions promoted by Fred Bannister and Norman Dickens on Thursday nights. Other name groups did appear at the Town Hall in the years to come, but this was the last of a sequence of gigs that began in October 1963.

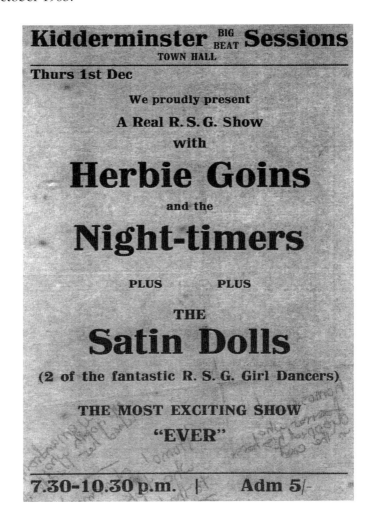

Friday 2nd December

The estimated cost of the ring road was announced as 3 million pounds, and that there were 126 objections to the scheme.

In the same issue an article appeared about a local eighteen-year old Robert Plant who at the time lived at Causey Farm Road, Hayley Green. Robert was vocalist with Midland group 'Listen'; they had just had their first single released on CBS entitled *'You Better Run'*. The group got their influences from obscure black American LPs. Robert reckoned the group played as loud as 'The Who'. He had previously sung with local blues outfit 'The Crawling Kingsnakes'.

'The Secrets' also announced they had a new single out on CBS this week, called '*I Suppose*', thanks to independent record producer Eddie Trevett who picked up on them via some demos they had earlier done for Jimmy Page.

Saturday 17th December

Arlo Guthrie, son of the legendary American folk singer Woody Guthrie, appeared at the Galleon Folk Club in Stourport.

Saturday 24th December

Chris Farlow and the Thunderbirds appeared at Stourport Civic, supported by 'The Secrets'.

New Year's Eve

The year finished with 'The Secrets' headlining a New Year's Eve gala at Stourport Civic, while 'Tommy and the Crestas' saw out the year at the Park Attwood.

1967

Friday 20th January

An interesting article appeared in the Shuttle, which told the story of ghostly goings on at the Black Horse. Way back in the seventeenth century the then landlord shot dead his wife and her lover, a coachman. Since then the wife had been haunting the old coaching inn. Things were particularly bad just before Christmas. The licensees at the time, Mr and Mrs Steadman, at first thought they had intruders but none were ever found. The odd job man there, Major Fell, was even touched on the head by a ghost. The article also mentioned that the Black Horse itself would soon be a thing of the past, as it stood in the way of the new ring road.

Friday 27th January

The Beat Scene column, written by Malcolm Nicholl, had now changed its name to On the Inside, and featured an article on an appearance by Jimmy Cliff and 'The Shakedown Sound' at the Black Horse the previous Thursday. The article wrote that a dynamic Jimmy Cliff really entertained an unusually lively Kidderminster crowd, with the 'Shakedowns', including local musicians Kevyn Gammond and Sean Jenkins, providing a solid foundation. Also mentioned was the previous Friday's all-nighter at the Chateau, which featured the 'Protection Racket' from Worcester, and local blues outfit 'Chicken Shack'. Another great night with a full house.

Friday 3rd February

The famous baritone saxophonist Ronnie Ross made an appearance at the Worcester Cross Hotel for Kidderminster Jazz Club. At the Playhouse was the famous play '*The Killing of Sister George*'. It had an all female cast who used a lot of unlady-like invective. It was advertised as not suitable for children.

Friday 17th February

On the Inside featured an article on the 'Apper Clarse' and their tour of Germany. Based in Kiel, the group also played in Dortmund and around Schleswig and Luneberg. They were in Germany for eight weeks and thoroughly enjoyed their experience. More work was offered to them but they declined. They did bring back from Germany some souvenirs, giant sausages! In the same issue it was announced that 'The Secrets' were releasing a new single on CBS on the 24th; both Cliff Ward compositions. The A-side was '*Infatuation*' with '*Dangerous*' on the B-side.

Friday 24th February

On the Inside featured a long article on 'The Alan Bown Set's appearance at Kidderminster College on Wednesday, February 15th for a Valentine's Dance. Headlined "The Alan Bown Set Delight and Amaze", and they did, fronted by Jess Roden on vocals, the seven-piece band created an energetic and dynamic performance. With band leader Alan Bown on trumpet and John Antony on sax they got a full-house crowd into a great party mood, with a whole gang of girls joining the band on stage at the end of the set.

Friday 24th March

Under the headlines "Friday Night and Saturday Morning", Malcolm Nicholl wrote about an 'all-niter' he had been to the previous Friday.

He said early risers in Kidderminster were surprised to see hundreds of sleepy teenagers walking through the town centre on Saturday morning. They had just returned by coach from an 'all-niter at the Chateau. First band on were 'The Frame' followed by 'Chicken Shack' a trio at this time, they were praised for their power house Chicago Blues. Later on another band turned up and played an impromptu set. The 'all-niter' was turning out to be a real cultural phenomenon.

Friday 31st March
During the previous week the statue of Richard Baxter had been removed from its place in the Bull Ring to be re-sited on the outer ring road near to St. Mary's Church.

Friday 7th April
An article described how the Royal George pub in Hall Street had been left in splendid isolation, due to the new ring road. It was not to survive much longer.

Wednesday 26th April
Robert Plant and the 'Band of Joy' appeared at the newly opened Casa Fiesta Disco, which took place at the Crown in Stourport.

Friday 5th May
The Beat Scene column was bemoaning the fact that the Town Hall had stopped putting name bands on and that the Stourport Civic was failing to attract large crowds in spite of acts like Wayne Fontana, Dave Berry, Chris Farlow and Screaming Lord Sutch appearing there. It was also reported that 'Ronnie Jones and the Q Set' stood in for 'Herbie Goins' at the Chateau and was an excellent replacement.

Friday 19th May
The official opening of the ring road had taken place the previous week. 'Out with the old and in with the new' could have been the headlines, as it was also announced that the Oaklands, a fine old house on Chester Road North that had served in recent years as Tomkinson's Social Club, had been demolished that week. It was also reported that on Tuesday night at Frank Freeman's there was a great double bill with both Robert Plant and his new group 'Band Of Joy' and Jimmy Cliff and 'The Shakedown Sound' appearing. It was reported as one of the best sessions for a long time. Robert Plant and

the 'Band of Joy' were also booked to appear at the 'all-niter' at the Chateau that night.

Friday 3rd June
On the Inside column announced new singles from both Jimmy Cliff, '*I Got A Feeling*', and 'The Secrets': '*I Intend To Please*' another one of Cliff Ward's own compositions.

Friday 30th June
On the Inside reported that 400 people turned up to see 'The Alan Bown Set' at Stourport Civic Centre on Wednesday night for the college dance in spite of the fact that someone had overlooked to book a licensed bar; soft drinks only were available on the night. Also that week the ultimate trendy 60s film was showing at the ABC from July 2nd: '*Blow Up*' with Vanessa Redgrave, David Hemmings and Sara Miles. The following Sunday the classic spaghetti-western '*A Fistful of Dollars*' with Clint Eastwood was at the ABC.

Friday 4th July
Malcolm Nicholl wrote in his Beat Scene '67 column that he had met a sixteen-year old would-be hippie who asked him why he didn't write more about the West Coast scene. The young lad was dressed in a flowered shirt, flared trousers with a medallion and beads draped round his neck, and was carrying some weeds (he couldn't find any flowers). He explained to Malcolm that the West Coast hippies were against violence; they preached about love, happiness, peace and goodwill to all men and that they expressed themselves by staging gigantic love-ins and through their music, everything must be beautiful. The essence of 'flower power' very well explained, and certainly right on the ball, with the local top ten showing '*All You Need Is Love*' by 'The Beatles' at number 1 and Scott McKenzie's '*San Francisco*' at number 6. Other records in the local charts were 'The Turtles' '*She'd Rather Be With Me*' at number 2, '*See Emily Play*' by 'Pink Floyd' at 5, '*Groovin*' by the 'Young Rascals' at 7, 'The Small Faces' '*Here Comes the Nice*' at 8, '*Respect*' by Aretha Franklin, 9, and '*Carrie-Ann*' by 'The Hollies' at 10. Probably one of the hippest local charts ever; the summer of love of 1967 was definitely with us.

In the same article 'Wynder K Frogg' got a good review for his appearance at the Black Horse. He had also appeared on Thursday

July 13th at one of the new Thursday night sessions at the Chateau. The previous week 'The Long John Baldry Show' had been there, and future acts booked were John Mayall and 'Herbie Goins'. Wow!

Friday 28th July

In an interesting article in Beat Scene '67, a local promoter explained that the days of the Town Hall were finished, and the acts such as Wynder K Frogg, Graham Bond and John Mayall could fill out the Black Horse, creating a great atmosphere.

Saturday 29th July

The licensee of The Boat in Clensmore Street, Eric Turner, pulled the last pint in the 200 year-old pub which was due for demolition. One of the last customers there was Bert Taylor, better known as 'The Count', one of the Midlands' fastest beer drinkers, who downed a pint of mild in four seconds. Bert said he could normally drink it in two, but he was a little out of practice!

Friday 11th August

There was a report of John Mayall's 'Bluesbreakers' appearing at Malvern Winter Gardens, supported on the night by local group 'Custard Tree'. It was only their fifth gig; it said they showed great promise for such a new group.

Friday 24th August

Scene '67 featured an article on Kidderminster DJs Fizz and Nick (Anthony Woodhouse and Nick Clegg). They had become so popular DJ-ing at the Chateau 'all-niters' that they were given their own show at the Co-op Hall in Worcester. They were reported to be in London meditating over the many offers of work they had had from all over the country. Their next gig was to be at the Chateau on Friday September 8th when Jimmy Cliff and 'The Shakedown Sound', and 'Chicago Hush' were the acts booked to appear. It was also reported that Frank Freeman would be having a Flower Power Night on Saturday September 2nd.

Friday 1st September

Scene '67 reported that Thursday nights at the Black Horse would be "better group sessions". First up would be 'Long Stack Humphreys' on September 7th. It was also reported that DJ Rod Gilchrist and

Butch Humber were seen dueting with the 'Jamaican Menders' at the Black Horse the previous Thursday; the song, '*Midnight Hour*'. Also in the same issue of the Shuttle appeared an article on carpet firm Carpet Trades changing their name to Gilt Edge.

Friday 8th September

It was announced that stage two of the Inner Ring Road would start in March 1968. It would mean that the Kidderminster Playhouse would be demolished along with four pubs: The Worcester Cross Hotel, The Leopard, The West Midland Railway Inn and The Square and Compass. There was also a report on Frank Freeman's very first Flower Power night. There was a good turn out of Flower Children all dressed with beads and bells and flowers, the smell of incense was heavy in the air. Music was provided by 'Breakthru', who finished their set with a psychedelic 'freak-out'. Their drummer in fact passed out, but fortunately made a full recovery. The 'all-niters' started again at the Chateau with the return of Jimmy Cliff and 'The Shakedowns' who went down a storm to a full house.

The Alan Bown Set - Jess R oden singing
Photo: Colin Hill

Friday 13th October

The On the Inside column featured a report on 'The Alan Bown Set's appearance at Franks. They were said to have given a top class exhilarating performance. There was also an article on Kevyn

Gammond leaving the 'Shakedowns', to be replaced by Mick Ralphs from Bromyard on lead guitar. Kevyn was going to join Robert Plant's 'Band of Joy' on their return from a tour of Scotland. 'The Indigo Set' also announced a new line up with Joey Dunnett (ex-'Renegades') taking over on lead and Sam Connell (ex 'Suedes') taking over on bass.

Friday 3rd November
'The Drifters' appeared at the Chateau in the upstairs ballroom, although they didn't appear on stage until 4am on the Saturday morning. Backed by the 'London All Stars', they kicked off their set with '*On Broadway*' and performed many of their famous hits. The general consensus was that they put on a great show. Whether there were any original members of 'The Drifters' on stage nobody really knew apart from a local man, Michael Townley from Bliss Gate, who reckoned they were an American group called 'The Invitation' who had been touring the UK. They were managed by the same person who managed the original 'Drifters'; he even
named all the group members.

Tuesday 21st November
'Timebox' from London made a big impression at Frank's with their lead singer Mike Patto. It was also announced on Friday December 1st that the new agency in Kidderminster had started up run by Norman Dickens and Nigel Mills it was called NORSAN (after Nigel's wife Sandra).

Friday 8th December
On the Inside column told the story of PP Arnold, who was deputising for Felice Taylor at Franks. She actually drove to Kettering instead of Kidderminster. DJ Rod Gilchrist entertained the crowd all evening with records in her place.

Thursday 14th December
It was reported in the On the Inside column that the end of term college dance turned out to be a bit of a flop. Nobody wanted to know about the 'Tony Billingham Dance Band', the other main act, Robert Plant's 'Band of Joy', went down much better but they were hardly the kind of group you wanted to dance to with their West
Coast 'progressive rock'.

The 'all-niter' at the Chateau on Saturday/Sunday seemed a much more successful affair. 'Wynder K Frogg' and his brilliant organ playing and his group kept the packed crowd dancing all through the night. Wynder enjoyed his set so much he played for another hour in the morning, also on the bill was Jimmy Cliff and 'The Shakedowns'. Although they went down well enough, a slight waning in popularity was discerned. As usual Nick and Fizz kept the music going with their soul and ska records.

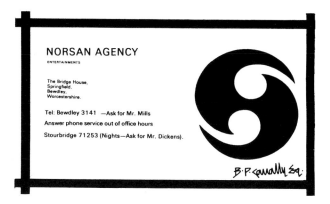

Friday 29th December

There was a sad ending to the year with the announcement that Harvey's Wine Lodge in Swan Street was to close and be demolished the following day. The building, owned by sherry producers and wine merchants Charles Harvey of Bristol had been built in 1790 although the cellars were much older, going back to medieval times. Part of them contained a subterranean chapel known as 'The Crypt' which was supposed to be linked to St Mary's Parish Church. Members of the Harvey family themselves had actually lived above the shop. John Harvey was there first in 1822, his brother Charles came up from Bristol and took over in 1840. None of these rather romantic and historical associations with the medieval church, the great seaport of Bristol and the Andalucian sherry town of Jerez made any impression on the soulless bureaucrats and venal property developers. One of them said "The retention of any buildings apart from Baxter's monument in the Bull Ring would seem to have little virtue, as they would seriously prejudice the execution of the overall redevelopment scheme" (The Swan Centre). Apart from Harvey's Wine Lodge, two buildings that were listed as having historical and architectural interest - the former Fox Inn and the building occupied by the Maypole Dairy - were also demolished, as was a favourite pub of mine, The Black Bull. This was vandalism of the highest order.

On the musical front, 1967 was a fantastic year, plenty of venues and different styles of music; you could see a live band every day of the week. Soul music was still very popular with the Stax and Motown sound predominant. There was also a big following by the mods for Blue Beat music, there was even a Blue Beat Top Five chart supplied by Long's record shop, courtesy of Brian Wilson, which was situated strategically between Frank Freeman's and the Black Horse. The chart on Friday April 21st had Desmond Dekker's – '007' at the number 1 spot.

But the really significant happening of the year was the arrival of the West Coast Sound from America which made its presence felt early in the year and was to change the course of rock and pop and usher in a whole new way of life. In the vanguard of this locally was Robert Plant's 'Band of Joy', but many more were to follow.

 The revolution had begun!

THE FRANK FREEMAN DANCING CLUB,
5, Mill Street, KIDDERMINSTER. Tel.No. 4118

PROUDLY PRESENTS..........SUNDAY, December 3rd.
The Greatest Atrraction .....In The Charts At. No. 8 ..
American Singing Star....FELICE TAYLOR.... FELICE TAYLO
FELICE TAYLOR And Her Backing Group .....FELICE TAYLOR.
Hear Her Sing, In Person, "I FEEL LOVE COMING ON"......
THIS SUNDAY, Dec. 3rd. THIS SUNDAY, Dec. 3rd. THIS S
7.15 - 10.30 p.m. Admission ... Members 8/6 ....Guests
Please Come Early..... Don't Miss This........

SUNDAY, December 10th.
From The Marquee Club, London, WARREN DAVIS MONDAY BANK
SUNDAY, December 17th.
London's "Deram", SKIP BIFFERTY, SKIP BIFFERTY. Adm.
SUNDAY, December 24th. Christmas Eve.
The Rave NEW GENERATION And THE STRINGBEATS. Adm. 8/6
MONDAY, December 25th. Christmas Day.
"SPIN-A-DISC" From 4.0 - 7.0 p.m. Adm. 3/6
TUESDAY, December 26th. Boxing Night.
The Up-Up Group ROBERT PLANT AND THE BAND OF JOY. Adm.
SUNDAY, December 31st. New Year's Eve.
Blues Best AYNSLEY DUNBAR RETALIATION. Adm. 6/6

THE BEST GROUPS   FOR THE BEST PEOPLE

ACKNOWLEDGEMENTS

I would like to thank the many people who have helped me in this chapter, they are:

Charles Talbot, Norman Dickens, Dave Bodley, Peter Phillips, Graham Pillon, Ken Swannell, John Carter, Paul Turner, Brian Wilson, Martin Stook, Butch Humber, Tony Goodwin, Dave Towers, George Kristic, Eve Deakin, Pete Longmore, Elmer O'Shea, Colin Youngjohns, Ian Hardiman, Martin Harrison, Joe Dunnett, Rob Newell, Nigel Knowles, Terry Edwards, Robert Plant, Bill Davies, Bob Barber, Phil Chadbourne, Stan Webb, Roger Sullivan, Lyn Sullivan, Alvar Spencer, Andy Silvester, Roger Capewell, Pete Waldron, Kevyn Gammond, Nigel Turrall, Nigel Bache, Trevor Jones, Fred Harvard, Paul Jennings, John Trickett.

RECOMMENDED READING

There Must Be A Better Way - Freddy Bannister
ISBN - 9455-490-6

Bittersweet - Dave Cartwright
ISBN - 1-901447-18-9
(Many thanks to Dave for his fine book on the life of Clifford T. Ward).

CHAPTER THREE
A ROMANTIC REVOLUTION
THE HIPPY YEARS
1968 - 1972

In the spring of 1968 I moved to London with Martin Harrison, former drummer with 'The Indigo Set'. After a couple of weeks of bed and breakfasts, and dossing down in a spare room of my uncles, we eventually managed to rent a bedsit in Cheniston Gardens, off Kensington High Street, just around the corner from Derry and Toms and John Barker's department stores. We both got jobs, but life was expensive in this highly fashionable part of London. With Kensington Palace and Hyde Park just a five minute walk away, we were breathing the same air as royalty and billionaire Arab sheiks. With only a minimum amount of disposable income, our lifestyles were different to say the least, but the tube was cheap, and walking was free! The atmosphere in London in 1968 was electric; there were soapbox revolutionaries on every street corner from Notting Hill to Marble Arch, with frequent demonstrations against theVietnam war. Walking along Ladbroke Grove was as exotic as any of the foreign ports I had travelled to during my days in the Merchant Navy.

The music scene was vibrant, and now and again we managed to get to the Marquee where I saw Robert Plant and his new group 'Led Zeppelin', billed on the night as 'The New Yardbirds'. We also travelled to many of the rock venues spread all over London, including The Fishmonger's Arms in Wood Green, where we saw some more local heroes in the form of the blues group 'Chicken Shack'. Nearer to our bedsit in Kensington we could walk over to Hyde Park and check out the free concerts, including one by 'Tyrannosaurus Rex' in June 1968 featuring Marc Bolan and Peregrine Took. We watched with delight and amazement at the Flower People, especially the girls with their garlands of flowers round their heads, dancing and skipping in the natural amphitheatre bordering the Serpentine. Little did I know that 'Tyrannosaurus Rex' had already played in Kidderminster at Frank Freeman's club a couple of months earlier, to a similarly dressed audience.

With all these new influences and excitement around me, the daily grind of getting on the tube at Kensington High Street to travel to Farringdon Road; the walk on up to the publishing house in Bowling Green Lane, passing the headquarters of the Communist daily paper the 'Morning Star' on the way, became more and more tedious as the weeks passed by. My hair had now grown down to my shoulders, and I was sporting a full Frank

Zappa moustache. Working as a clerk in the despatch office with a bunch of 'straights' only increased my desire to get on the road as soon as possible. Sitting on the tube, on the way to work I read about the May Revolution in Paris, and was convinced that the entire western industrial and military complex was soon to crash down around our ears, ushering in a paradise on earth, free love, free music, free everything. Nobody then could have foreseen the self-inflicted tragedy that would befall the country some eleven years later.

I had no idea that back in Kidderminster the very same things were happening. Not the political demonstrations - Kidderminster is only a small town after all - but you could buy a copy of The International Times, the hippy bible, at certain newsagents. The music scene was just as progressive as London's, if on a smaller scale. The epicentre of this musical revolution in Kidderminster, was Frank Freeman's Dancing Club. For three years from 1968 to 1971 it was one of the hippest rock venues in the entire UK. The rock gigs were on Sunday nights, the rest of the week Frank and Wynn Freeman taught Ballroom Dancing, everything from Old Tyme to Latin American and Tap.

Frank and Wynn met at a church hall dance in Leicester in 1940, during the war. They were married two years later, and moved to Frank's home town of Kidderminster in 1947. They both loved dancing and had trained as dance teachers. Their first dance school was at the New Meeting Church Hall opened in 1948. They were rather limited there, as they could only run classes two days a week, so Frank got a part time job as a book-keeper for Sid Simmonds, the butcher. Sid was the owner of a property in Lower Mill Street, which had once been the home of the Bijou Cinema, Kidderminster's first picture house, which ran until the advent of the First World War. When the premises became vacant at the end of 1955, Sid offered the lease to Frank. After much hard work, which included the removal of the balcony and the installation of a floor for dancing, the school was opened the first week of January 1956. During that first year an old lady came into the club and said that she remembered going there as a child, when it was also a variety hall as well as a cinema, and recalled seeing dancing bears perform there.

The Dance School was a great success. Frank often promoted the famous dance bands of the day at Kidderminster Town Hall; he put on Victor Sylvester, Joe Loss, and Edmundo Ross, amongst others. When rock 'n' roll started, Frank and Wynn were soon off the mark, running jiving classes and eventually putting on rock 'n' roll groups on Sunday nights. One of Wynn's favourites were 'The Deltas' from Birmingham.

The mod scene started at Frank's in 1965. A group of ten people, Rod Gilchrist, Nick Clegg and David Shuck, amongst others, used to travel regularly to the Whiskey club in Birmingham, where they picked up on soul music and mod fashion. This small group stuck together at Frank's, where they attracted the attention of rockers who also used to frequent the Flamingo Café next door. The mods had been threatened by the rockers, that they were "Going to get beaten up next Sunday". So the Kidderminster mods spread the word at the next Saturday all-nighter at the Whiskey, and about 200 mods turned up at Frank's on the Sunday. When the rockers tried to get into Frank's for a ruckus, they were shocked to see so many mods, so they turned round and left. From then on Sundays were mod sessions. Frank put on blue beat and soul acts from Birmingham such as 'The Stringbeats' and the 'Jamaican Nobles'. This lasted until the summer of love 1967, when things almost changed overnight and some of the new young hippies were, in their turn, occasionally set on by die-hard mods. Frank once again was

FRANK FREEMAN

tuned into the current trends. He soon began booking what were known as underground or progressive groups, with a few tips and encouragement from DJ Rod Gilchrist, and Robert Plant and Kevyn Gammond from the 'Band of Joy', who were one of the new breed of groups to appear. Rod Gilchrist became almost evangelical about his new music, astonishing his mod friends when he invited them around to his house, when his parents were away. He played the *'Forever Changes'* LP by 'Love' and other West Coast groups all night, to their utter amazement.

The change in music and fashion, from mods to hippies, also involved a change in the drug culture. The mods essentially used drugs to keep them awake, in order to dance all night; uppers in the form of French Blues, Green Clears and Dexys. With the advent of progressive rock and hippy culture, people were chilling out more, listening to music rather than dancing. A more contemplative ambience was required. Hallucinogenic drugs became very popular, particularly cannabis, but also LSD "To expand your mind and unlock your hidden consciousness"; it was a very cool thing to do. As

Kidderminster was a real hotspot for music, it inevitably became a hotspot for drugs. Vans would turn up in town on gig nights. With their fur-lined interiors, they dispensed their wares to a young and expectant clientele. For most of the youngsters this was an exciting and exploratory time, but there were casualties. Excessive usage and dangerous combinations, sometimes with alcohol, led an unfortunate few to serious damage and even death.

At the beginning of 1968, some now famous bands started appearing at Frank's. Peter Green's 'Fleetwood Mac' had gone down a storm in January, and John Peel himself brought 'Tyrannosaurus Rex' up to Frank's for an all nighter on Easter Sunday, after he had broadcast his Top Gear radio show on Sunday afternoon. In those days, Marc Bolan and Peregrine Took were

CAPTAIN BEEFHEART
at Frank Freeman's
Photo by Colin Hill

very short of money, and DJs Paul 'Pig' Jennings and Rod Gilchrist put them up for the night in their respective parent's houses.

On Sunday May 19th, 'Captain Beefheart and his Magic Band' made their legendary appearance at Frank's. When John Peel told the band the name of their next gig was Frank Freeman's Dancing Club, they said "What a groovy name". John Peel said it wasn't a groovy name, it was a dance club run by a bloke called Frank Freeman! John Peel drove the Captain (Don

Van Vliet) and drummer, John French, up to Frank's after broadcasting his radio programme. This was the only Midlands' date, and one of the very few in the country, that Captain Beefheart played. Wynn Freeman remembers them arriving, wearing very large stovepipe hats. The Captain asked Wynn if they served alcohol. When the answer was no, he replied "Thank God for that", and took off his hat and explained to Wynn and Frank that at some of the places they played they had bottles thrown at them. They then all sat down with Wynn and Frank to cups of tea and cucumber sandwiches, with the crusts cut off. The band enjoyed this homely touch. The Captain had a few games of pinball at the Flamingo Café next door, and checked out the local shoe shops. He apparently fell in love with a pair of boots, which were only available in England, and eventually had a pair sent to the States.

On the night, the place was packed to the hilt. People were standing outside listening, the band was so loud you could just about follow the set. The Captain played his famous reed instrument, the shenai, that had been given to him by Ornette Coleman, and held the enthusiastic young audience spellbound; no walkouts. For some reason John Peel turned up late during the set and had trouble getting in the door, as the doorman didn't recognise him. He set up a tape recorder, and the last four numbers of the set were recorded for prosterity. They were *'Rollin' 'n' Tumblin'*, *'Electricity'*, *You're Gonna Need Somebody On Your Bond'* and *'Kandy Korn'*. These tracks later appeared in a rarities 5 CD album called *'Grow Fins'*. After *'Kandy Korn'*, Captain Beefheart can be heard saying "Thank you very much folks". 'The Magic Band' line up on the night was: Don Van Vliet, vocals and reed instruments; Alex St. Clair, guitar; Jeff Cotton, guitar; Jerry Handley, bass and John French, drums.

PETER GREEN
Photo by Colin Hill

Other well-known visitors that Wynn remembers well include Rick Wakeman. During one of his sessions when the audience were shouting for encores, Rick's amp blew up and brought a swift end to the show. Once when 'The Strawbs' played at Frank's on a Sunday afternoon, they followed

DJ Paul Jennings down to the Wharf in the evening, where he did some DJing and helped Rob Baynham out with his light show. Rick Wakeman and Dave Cousins bought a lot of drinks that night. Wynn also remembers Peter Green. When she commented on how quickly they set up and sound checked, he replied "Why not, they should know what they're doing by now". He also once returned £10 to Frank, saying he had been overpaid. In spite of Frank insisting it was correct, the £10 was returned to him.

Another of Wynn's favourites was Robert Plant. Frank and Wynn always had a party on either Christmas Day or Boxing Day, between 2pm and 8pm. Robert would always turn up with his family, and stay from start to finish. 'Bronco' with Jess Roden on vocals, would supply the live music, and Robert would normally sing at least a half-hour set. This was at the height of his fame with 'Led Zeppelin'. When a tribute gig had been arranged at the Gainsborough following Frank Freeman's death, Robert interrupted vital rehearsal sessions for a Freddy Mercury tribute concer, that was due to be held at Wembley, to attend the memorial show at the Gainsborough.

These famous rock sessions finished in 1971 when the groups became very famous and too expensive. Bands like 'Yes' for example, would honour bookings far below their normal fee, but eventually the gigs stopped. The groups were well beyond the price that Frank could afford. The ballroom dancing carried on as normal, and Frank still put the occasional dance band on at either Kidderminster Town Hall or Stourport Civic Centre. Victor Sylvester and Joe Loss were both booked by Frank in 1972.

While preparing for a children's party on October 27th, 1991, Frank collapsed and died in his beloved Dance Club. Over the years he had gained the respect of everyone he met, whether they were avant-garde musicians from California or young mums bringing their kids in for tap dancing. Frank treated them all the same. The occasional drunk that would wander in would be gently escorted to the Coach and Horses next door, and told to come again on another night. A gentleman in the true sense of the word. He had an open mind to any sort of music, although his great love was dancing. He was rather puzzled that the youngsters would rather sit down and listen than dance, but he accepted things as they were.

The usual Christmas party went ahead that year; the club was packed to the hilt, with Robert Plant there from beginning to end. So think, next time you walk past the studded door surrounded by white tiles with the famous Dance Club* sign above, of everything that has gone on there, from dancing bears to silent movies, and ballroom dancing to acts such as 'Captain Beefheart', 'Tyrannosaurus Rex' and 'Fleetwood Mac'.

Meanwhile back in the summer of 1968 in London, Martin Harrison eventually got a drummer's job with 'The Hi-Fi's', a pop group who were 'Big in Germany'. Later in November their road manager left. This was the

chance I had been waiting for. A quick trip up to Kidderminster secured me a second hand Ford Transit, and my first job as a road manager. The first trip to Germany included a residency at the Bonanza Club in Dortmund, and a trip to the Star Club in Hamburg. Further trips to Germany followed, including a riotous week in Munchen Gladbach during their pre-Lent festivities, when the whole town parties for a week; great fun. 'The Hi-Fi's' split up in March, and I worked freelance for a bit, including a number of gigs for Jamaican reggae star Jackie Edwards (writer of *Keep on Running*). I also did quite a few transport jobs for Jackie Edwards's bass player Phil Chen,a great bassist who later worked with Rod Stewart in his glory days, and also, by coincidence, with Jess Roden in 'The Butts Band'.

I eventually got an emergency call to take the backing band of 'The Fantastics' to Germany. "When do you want me?", "Now", was the reply. So throwing a few things in an overnight bag, I was off to Germany once more. This was a short tour of American bases. 'The Fantastics' were a four piece black vocal group from New York. Don, John, Richie and Romie; great singers, the real business. They had originally come over to the UK to tour as 'The Fantasic Temptations', but eventually got fed up with having writs served on them and went out under their own name of 'The Fantastics'. Their English backing group hailed from various parts of west London. The core of the group was Pip Williams on lead guitar, and Ron Thomas on bass.

After this initial German trip, the band spent May gigging in the UK and then it was back to Germany. This time we had a permanent base in Frankfurt, and gigged all over the US bases in the area, as far south as

Stuttgart. After the gig while the band usually headed back to the hotel, me and the other roadie, Pete, went to the well known K52 rock club in the Kaiserstrasse. It was there one night that I found out that Linda, the girl singer in the club band, actually came from Kidderminster.

From Frankfurt we did a one-off gig at a naval base in Italy. Before we left Frankfurt for France, the Australian agent there offered me a permanent job escorting the acts around the bases for the Deutschmark equivalent of £50 per week. It was a tempting offer but there was a problem, I had to get my hair cut and wear white overalls. So it was a case of "Thanks, but no thanks". From Frankfurt we went to a luxury nightclub in the hills behind Cannes, called the Akou Akou. From there we headed for Barcelona and onwards to Palma, Majorca, and a two-month residency at Club Sloopy. Unbeknown to me, my destiny was unfolding, for it was in Sloopys that I met Brigitte Bardot look-alike Hazel Strandberg, all the way from the pine forests of northern Sweden. Working at Sloopys was a cushy number, all I had to do was take a taxi to the club every night, connect the mics and get a sound balance. Rehearsals were twice a week when I had to turn out in the afternoons. I was on £45 a week for this less than arduous task; the rest of the time was my own.

Unfortunately our two month stay was cut short when one of 'The Fantastics' got too interested in a local Spanish girl, daughter of a police chief. We were unceremoniously thrown off the island with another month left of our contract. My time in paradise was up.

After a short spell in Malvern (Mother had moved there in 1968), I was back in London freelancing. 'The Fantastics' had problems with work permits, having come back to the UK too soon. So I joined up once again with Pip Williams and Ron Thomas in a soul jazz band called 'Sweetwater Canal', managed from Ronnie Scott's jazz club in Soho, where we were based. To help make ends meet, we got the job backing Arthur Conley ('*Sweet Soul Music*') on a UK tour in November 1969, followed by another tour with him, which began in January 1970. This time Arthur Conley was part of a soul package tour which also included Joe Tex, Clarence Carter and the very wonderful Sam and Dave. Orange supplied the PA and back line, all I had to look after was a drum kit. Unfortunately on the Manchester Odeon gig, their transport failed to arrive, so I was sent to Swan's music shop in Manchester to get equipment. It was all nicely set up when I noticed that there was no fuse in the bass amp. Drastic measures were required with the audience already getting into their seats. So I ripped up some foil paper from a cigarette packet and shoved it in the fuse holder; power on, show on. I watched from the wings. Sam and Dave had two drummers and put on a great show. Apparently in ordinary life they didn't get on well, but on stage they were dynamite together. In thanks for helping them out of an emergency situation, I got invited by the agents to a nightclub in Manchester with them and Arthur Conley; I never mentioned the cigarette paper.

We also did another tour later on in the year with Arthur Conley, together with Percy Sledge, Desmond Dekker and Max Romeo ('*Wet Dreams*'); the 'Soul meets Reggae' tour, with Johnny Walker as compere. Somewhere along the line I remember Arthur wanted to have a few beers in a real English pub, but he was a bit worried about the race issue. Coming from the deep south of America, in those days it was a real fear for him. Anyway we found a pub, Arthur got his beer and asked for some fried eggs "Sunny side up". Nobody understood what he meant, including the barmaid, but he managed to explain and we all had a good laugh. He was a real nice easy-going guy. When that tour finished Arthur returned to the States, and 'Sweetwater Canal' went out on their own. It was during this period that I came into contact with 'The Crazy World of Arthur Brown'. My van had broken down after a gig at Rebecca's in Birmingham, and through an agent, Clive Wilson, Arthur Brown's roadie came up and helped out with transport. He also needed help and asked me to give him a hand with Arthur Brown, I agreed. One gig with Arthur I remember really well was a Festival of Peace and Love at Victoria Park in Hackney. A bunch of skinheads had turned up and started causing trouble. As I was setting the Hammond organ up, I noticed beer bottles flying around me. Arthur started the show with his famous 'Hellfire Helmet' on. As the crowd got increasingly disruptive Arthur reportedly lifted his magical cape exposing himself to the audience, calling the troublemakers "A bunch of wankers". After that, all hell broke loose, apparently the Hell's Angels chased the skinheads into the park pond and a huge fight ensued. The show was brought to a swift halt and we quickly broke the gear down, beer bottles still raining on stage. We were escorted away from the park by Hell's Angels on their bikes. Hazel had just arrived from Sweden and had met me there; what a welcome!

After every gig with Arthur we had to drive the gear down to Puddletown in Dorset, where Arthur lived in some style in the wings of a fine old mansion house. We then had to drive home to London. Arthur was always very polite and friendly but the trips back to London were becoming increasingly wearing. So one night, after another mad gig at the Brighton Dome where 'Hawkwind' were also on the bill - and students stormed the stage dressed as French revolutionaries re-enacting the battle of the Bastille - Clive, the head roadie, decided to become revolutionary against his employers and threw some of the gear around. One major bugbear had been drummer Drachen Theaker's kit. His knackered old bass pedal frequently came off, whereupon he usually lobbed it at one of us standing in the wings. Needless to say, Clive finished with Arthur that night so that was me finished as well. A great experience, I remained friends with Clive for quite some time and we kept in touch for years.

After a gig with 'Sweetwater Canal', backing Doris Troy at The Place in Hanley, the band split up and I had a short spell freelancing again. I had a trip to the continent with rock band 'Quatermass' with ex 'Undertakers' and 'Mersey's' Johnny Gustaffson on bass. The tour included Sweden where I met up with Hazel again in Stockholm.

In September 1970, after a short spell with folk rock group 'Storyteller', I was back on the soul circuit, as Pip Williams had got together a group to back Jamaican soul singer 'Jimmy James and the Vagabonds'. Jimmy was another great singer and the band worked solidly until June 1971. At Worcester College of Further Education, Jimmy James headlined on the main stage while a young band supported us playing their set on the dance floor. We all thought they were really good; they were called 'Genesis'.

At the beginning of June, the backing group did a short tour with Jimmy Ruffin (*"What Becomes Of The Brokenhearted"*). One of the gigs was at Chesford Grange in Kenilworth where the DJ thought he was the star of the show. He had plugged his gear, including flashing lights, into our plug board. With less than ten minutes to go till Jimmy Ruffin came on, I asked the DJ politely if he could finish his set, three or four times, but he totally ignored me. I thought 'Bollocks to this' and promptly whipped out all his plugs and put mine in, whereupon I was seized by two bouncers and dragged outside for a severe beating. I explained to them that if I couldn't get back to the stage, Jimmy Ruffin wouldn't appear. They reluctantly let me go and the show went ahead. The final gig of the tour was at Oakengates Town Hall. It was also my final gig: I decided to call it a day. Hazel had moved in with me and I had problems with insurance on the van amongst other things. Of course this was just a temporary measure, I reasoned with myself.

I took on a driving job with two wonderfully eccentric marine antique dealers in Hampstead. This lasted until the spring of 1973 when Hazel became pregnant. My mother had been ringing from home asking me to take over the family business with a decent flat thrown in with the job. The decision wasn't too hard to make. Our rather bohemian flat in Kilburn was no place to bring up a baby, so the die was cast. All our worldly goods were packed into the back of the Transit, and without a second glance, we left the Canterbury Arms car park, drove down Kilburn Lane to the White City, along the Great Western Avenue onto the A40, and headed home to Kidderminster.

*Since writing the dance club signed has been removed prior to refurbishment

THE GROUPS
1968 – 1972

Bartholomews Creed - Deaf Cuckoo - Bonehead

Bluesberry Hill - Freckles

Breakdown

CHICKEN SHACK

Liquorice - Mad Dog - BRONCO

ROBERT PLANT

The Reflections

Slamhammer

CLIFFORD T. WARD

Wise Virgin

BARTHOLOMEWS CREED/DEAF CUCKOO/BONEHEAD

1968 - 1971

'Bartholomew's Creed' were Elmer O'Shea, lead guitar; Johnny King, vocals; Paul Hyde, drums; Richie McGowan, bass, and 'Slim' O'Neil, saxophones. Formed in 1968, they were mainly a covers band who split up early in 1969. Elmer, Paul and Richie then formed 'Deaf Cuckoo' who were later joined by Butch Humber on vocals. They were a progressive rock group who wrote their own numbers. They supported 'The Nice' at Malvern Winter Gardens and 'Earth' (later 'Black Sabbath') at the Wharf, where Elmer was sounded out to join them on lead guitar. However Tony Iommi returned from 'Jethro Tull' and nothing became of it. After supporting 'Hawkwind' at Mothers in Birmingham, they were offered management by Wayne Bardell of Clearwater Management but they split up shortly afterwards.

Not long after this, bass player Terry Edwards knocked on Elmer's door and asked if he wanted to form a group. This band became 'Bonehead', with Colin 'Nobby' Hawkins on drums and Martin Lee on vocals. Martin Lee was soon replaced by ex 'Band of Joy' member Paul Lockey on rhythm guitar and vocals. 'Bonehead' wrote most of their own material, somewhat in the vein of 'Wishbone Ash'. They were the first band to play at JB's in Dudley and also supported 'Free' at the Wharf. When they supported 'The Troggs' at a private party in Wales, the businessman organising the party decided to pay them £500, the same as 'The Troggs', on the basis that they made the same racket. They were eventually managed by Wayne Bardell from Clearwater Management who got them lots of gigs in London, including the famous Speakeasy Club.

In 1971, they had a recording session at Island Studios thanks to 'Bronco' who had got them studio time. Jess Roden engineered the session. Unfortunately nothing happened with this and the band split up later in 1972. Elmer O'Shea went on to join Worcester group 'Pahana'.

Pahana
Far Left: Elmer O'Shea

166

BLUESBERRY HILL – FRECKLES

1968 - 1970

When 'The Indigo Set' split up early in 1968, it wasn't long before bass guitarist Rob Newell formed a new group. While talking to guitarist Tony Hill in the Swan with Two Nicks in Worcester, they decided to start a blues group. Tony brought in Worcester drummer Nick Brown while Rob brought in 'Butch' Humber on vocals and harmonica. They called the band 'Bluesberry Hill' and began rehearsing in the tin shack in Broadwaters, where the Rose Theatre now stands. After a few months of rehearsals the group started to gig successfully, but Tony Hill, always an enigmatic character, decided to buck the current trend and wanted to pack up the blues in order to play more commercial music on the club circuit. So one night in Brinton's Beacon Club, after only five or six gigs, Tony left the group and the band folded. Not long after Rob, with ex 'Raiders' drummer Chris Hayes and Jim Boden on guitar, joined up with Barry Dunn, vocals, and Gary Tolley, guitar; both from Stourbridge. They were a vocal harmony group in the style of 'The Beach Boys' called 'Freckles' and played extensively all over the Black Country and several tours of Wales. The band lasted about two years, when Rob got married and they eventually split up. In later years, Rob went on to play with the 'Stubble Brothers' and 'Slowburner'.

THE BREAKDOWN
1968 – 1972

'The Breakdown' originally started way back in 1963 when Dave Bradley, Roy Bragan and Alan Millward, all pupils at Stourport Secondary Modern, decided to form a group which they called 'The Soundbreakers', inspired by local heroes Cliff Ward and the Cruisers. They started playing local village halls and youth clubs and in 1966 added another guitarist, Richard Daminsky. Although an excellent guitarist he had to leave because he cut half an inch off his middle finger with a bacon slicer. They were then joined by vocalist Roger Hughes. Alan Millward rejoined them on drums after a short spell with 'The Reflections'. With the addition of Brian Stokes as manager, they changed their name to 'The Breakdown' in March 1968.

Not long after that, keyboard player Steve Coleman joined them and they started gigging regularly. They played at the Black Horse, the Chateau and many other venues locally and throughout the rest of the Midlands, mainly thanks to Norman Dickens and Nigel Mills of the NORSAN agency. Their set consisted of cover versions anything from '*Love Potion No. 9*' to 'Steppenwolf's '*Born to be Wild*', or '*Light my Fire*' by 'The Doors'. This was all in the middle of the psychedelic era. They decided to project some moving oil slides using candle fat and Duckhams oil, with the help of an old projector, two long bamboo poles and a white sheet. They tried this out first at Droitwich Winter Gardens where everyone stared incredulously at the stage, but it somehow worked. During 1969 Richard Hughes took over on drums and his brother Terry replaced Steve on keyboards. Terry brought with him a L100 Hammond and Leslie cabinet. The organ took four people to lift it and one time survived a thirty-foot drop from an icy iron staircase, after a gig in Bridgnorth.

"Breakdown" is the name a new Stourport group

l to r
Roy Bragan, Alan Millward, Dave Bradley, Roger Hughes.

They had some good gigs in 1969, including supporting 'Ten Years After' at

Malvern Winter Gardens and 'The Kinks' at Old Hill Plaza. Later on there were personnel changes, Derek Thomas joined on guitar. He was a really good guitarist who later went on to play on Clifford T Ward's albums. They were also joined by Bill Dancock on bass. Derek eventually left and was replaced by ex -'Cruisers' and 'Reflections' guitarist Graham Drew. Graham rejoined 'The Reflections' in 1972 and was replaced by original guitarist Dave Bradley. But the times were changing; discos were taking over from groups, so the band moved into a more cabaret style. With the change of style came a change of name to 'Haze', named inadvertently by Norman Dickens after a smoke filled pub they were sitting in, in Stourbridge. They are still playing locally with the name of 'pHAZE 2.'

BLACK
HORSE HOTEL, KIDDERMINSTER

*

FRIDAY, 1st NOVEMBER
BREAKDOWN

SATURDAY, 2nd NOVEMBER
MODELLE UNION

SUNDAY, 3rd NOVEMBER
TOMMY AND THE CRESTAS

TUESDAY, 5th NOVEMBER
JOE COCKER
AND THE
GREASE BAND

LICENSED BAR   8.00—11.00 p.m.

CHICKEN SHACK
1966 -

In January 1968, 'Chicken Shack' released their first single on the Blue Horizon label, '*It's OK With Me Baby*'. They also had their first session for Radio One on 'Top Gear' that month, one of many over the next few years. They gigged extensively throughout this period. With Christine on piano and vocals and Stan's exciting guitar playing, they were building a growing reputation, with long queues forming wherever they played. In July they recorded their first album at the CBS studios just off Bond Street, called '*Forty Blue Fingers Freshly Packed And Ready to Serve.*' They added a brass section in the form of Dick Heckstall -Smith, John Almond and Alan Ellison. The album was well received and reached number 2 in the charts. The band were now spending most of their time in London. Andy and Christine, together with Fleetwood Mac roadie Hugh Price from Kidderminster, shared a flat together in Holland Road. In fact members of 'Fleetwood Mac' were frequent visitors and they spent a lot of time listening to records together. In August Christine married bassist John McVie after he had proposed to her in the famous Bag O'Nails Club.

In October 1968, they recorded their second album '*OK Ken?*' before embarking on a two week tour of Scandinavia. In spite of exorbitant drink prices, they managed a riotous evening out with Stan throwing thousands of petals from fresh flowers all over manager Harry Simmonds in a very

l to r. Dave Bidwell, Christine Perfect,
Stan Webb, Andy Silvester

plush nightclub. They were threatened with being thrown out, but things calmed down and they had their last drink at six in the morning back in the hotel. The Album *'OK Ken?'* had a large horn section and also included Americas blues harmonica player Walter 'Shakey' Horton, as well as Stan doing his impersonations of various personalities such as John Peel and Kenneth Williams.

'OK Ken?' was released in February 1969, the same month that Stan married Andy Silvester's sister, Lyn. The album sold well, but their couple of singles had not done so well.

Early in 1969 they went into the studio to do a version of the Etta James number *'I'd Rather Go Blind'*; a rather different song for Christine to attempt, but she made a good job of it with her strong, melodic vocals. Andy Silvester helped her out on the Hammond organ by sitting beside her and pressing the bass pedals, then playing the electric bass as overdubs, giving the record a thick bass sound. Also at the session that day was Bobby Parker who had just flown in from America. They had a jam session with him and played *'Reconsider Baby'* amongst other numbers. The single was a hit and reached number 14 in the charts. The downside was that Christine left the band, although she appeared with them on their Top of the Pops performance. Christine had decided that being on the road with

Christine Perfect.
Mick Fleetwoods Flat, Montpellier Road, Ealing.
Photo: Clive Limpkin

'Chicken Shack' was incompatible with married life. Even so, she won the Melody Maker female vocalist of the year in 1969 and soon after she joined 'Fleetwood Mac' and won worldwide fame with them during the 1970s. Undeterred 'Chicken Shack' carried on with a new keyboard player Paul Raymond who was formerly with pop group 'Plastic Penny'. He refused to do an audition but got the job anyway and was a good addition musically to the band.

They recorded their third album *'100 Ton Chicken'* in April 1970 and released a single from it *'Tears In The Wind'* in August, which charted at 29. The album was released in September to critical acclaim. The horn section had been dropped and they had a much heavier sound, but sales were quite poor, the blues boom was slowing down. However they were still going down well live. Stan had acquired a hundred foot guitar lead which he used to good effect at the Bath Festival in the summer of 1969, when he went walkabout in the audience. On one famous occasion at the Speakeasy, Stan walked to the bar and had a drink while still playing his guitar solo. On another occasion he entertained the crowd single-handed at Birmingham Town Hall when the band's van broke down on their way from London.

In July 1970, they released their fourth album *'Accept'*, a much rockier album than before. From it they put out a very commercial single *'Maudie'*, but both failed to chart. In August they had a successful tour of America together with the 'Savoy Brown Blues Band' with whom they shared the same manager, Harry Simmonds. They played a huge open air festival in Dubuque, Iowa to 42,000 people and both Bill Graham's Fillmore East and Fillmore West in New York and San Francisco, as well as the Whisky-a-Go-Go in Los Angeles. This was followed by a short tour of Germany in November, but in December the group split up. Paul Raymond and Dave Bidwell left to

CHRISTINE AND ANDY
Blowup Club, Munich
Photo: Bernd Thiele

CHICKEN SHACK
l to r. Stan Webb, Paul Raymond, Andy Silvester, Dave Bidwell

join 'Savoy Brown', shortly followed by Andy Silvester.   Andy then contacted ex-'Redcaps' vocalist Dave Walker to join 'Savoy Brown'.

Andy stayed with them for a couple of years and had quite a few tours of America. Since then he has played in numerous bands including   Melvyn's Marauders, Ricky Cool & The Rialtos, Robert Plant's original 'Honeydrippers' and The Steve Gibbons Band In 1984 he went on to co-found 'The Big Town Playboys' with Ricky Cool. Andy now tours extensively with Mike Sanchez.

As for Stan Webb, he was in many line-ups, including a spell with Kim Simmonds in 'Savoy Brown'   recording the album *'Boogie Brothers'* in 1974. He also joined up with fellow Kidderminster guitarist Robbie Blunt, who made an album *'Broken Glass'* in 1975. But of course Stan is best known for devoting himself to 'Chicken Shack', carrying them forward into the new millennium, and the name with whom extrovert showman and guitar 'Stan the Man' will always be associated.

BILL GRAHAM PRESENTS IN NEW YORK

SMALL FACES
WITH
ROD STEWART
BLODWYN PIG
CHICKEN SHACK
PIG LIGHT SHOW
August 8, 1970

CHICKEN SHACK – DISCOGRAPHY
UK SINGLES

1967 *Its OK With Me Baby/When My Left Eye Jumps*
                                  Blue Horizon 57-3135
1967 *Worried About My Woman/Six Nights In Seven*
                                  Blue Horizon 57 – 3143
1968 *When The Train Comes Back/Hey Baby*
                                  Blue Horizon 57-3146
1969 *I'd Rather Go Blind/Night Life*
                                  Blue Horizon 57-3153
1969 *Tears In The Wind/The Things You Put Me Through*
                                  Blue Horizon 57-3168
1970 *Maudie/Andalucian Blues*
                                  Blue Horizon 57-3168
1970 *Sad Clown/Tired Eyes*
                                  Blue Horizon – 57-3176

UK ALBUMS

1968 *Forty Blue Finger, Freshly Packed And Ready To Serve*
                         Blue Horizon – 7-63203
1969 *OK Ken?*   Blue Horizon – 7-63209
1969 *100 Ton Chicken*   Blue Horizon – 7-63218
1970 *Accept*   Blue Horizon – 7-6386
1972 *Imagination Lady*   Deram SDL5

ACKNOWLEDGEMENTS

Rock 'n' Roll London – Max Woolridge
In Session Tonight   Ken Garner
Blues – Rock Explosion – Summer McStravick and John Roos
Chicken Shack Appreciation Society – Bonnie and Sue

Liquorice – Mad Dog – BRONCO
1968 – 1973

Young Wolverley guitarist Robbie Blunt, had played with 'Butch Clutch and the Accelerators', and a very short spell with 'Eddy and the Kings', before forming rock trio 'Liquorice' with ex-'Shakedown', Johnny Pasternak on bass and Dave Bodley on drums. They had their debut at Charles Talbot's fine old country house Honeybrook, where they played for charity in the summer of 1968. In October, Richard 'Mooney' Marzola joined them from Worcester group 'Rubber Duck'. They played local venues like Frank Freeman's and the Black Horse, but within six months they had split up. Robbie then got involved with ex-'Hellions' vocalist Gordon Jackson, who was working with Jim Capaldi, Chris Wood, Polly Palmer and Steve Winwood. First of all they rehearsed in Worcester, then Gordon's cottage in Martley, and in Jim Capaldi's flat in Cromwell Road, London. 'Rolling Stones' record producer, Jimmy Miller lived in the flat next door. Heady stuff for a young lad from Wolverley. Their album, produced by Dave Mason and called *'Thinking Back'*, was released on the Marmalade label. It didn't do too well and Robbie returned to Wolverley where, a short time after, he got a knock on the door from Kevyn Gammond and Jess Roden to join a new group which would eventually become 'Bronco'.

Kevyn Gammond & Johnny Pasternak in Rome 1969.

After the 'Band of Joy' split up, it wasn't long before Kevyn Gammond had formed a new group 'Mad Dog' which made its debut at Frank Freeman's, in October 1968. They played progressive rock with jazz influence. Although Kevyn said they were mostly "Muckin' about", they landed the job backing American jazz bluesman Jimmy Witherspoon and

Bronco l to r -
Johnny Pasternak, Jess Roden, Kevyn Gammond, Robbie Blunt, Pete Robinson

played all over the UK, including Ronnie Scott's jazz club in London. The line up was Kevyn Gammond, guitar, vocals; Paul Lockey, guitar/vocals; Johnny Pasternak, bass, and Colin 'Nobby' Hawkins, drums; augmented on Jimmy Witherspoon gigs with John Bishop, organ and Bryan Martin, sax. They got a lot of European work from Mike Dolan of the Terry King agency. On one trip to Berlin they played the Beautiful Balloon Club. Berlin at that time was a hotbed of revolutionary ideas and Kevyn, whose musical tastes had always been for raw powerful sounds, was totally knocked out by a recording he heard in Berlin by Peter Brotman. The LP titled '*Machine Gun Music*' had a pulverising explosive sound, recorded during street riots in Berlin and confirmed Kevyn's love of the avante-garde.

While touring in the UK with Jimmy Witherspoon, they were spotted by Italian pop star Tony Pinelli, who offered them a residency at the Piper Club in Rome. On their way to Rome they crashed into a lorry in Paris. The van was a total write-off and Nigel Pheysey, the roadie, was injured and returned to England. Tony Pinelli supplied a new Transit and they completed their journey to Rome. When they were in the Piper Club, they were joined on stage by jazz greats Ben Webster and Art Farmer doing numbers such as '*Tougher Than Tough*', and '*Ain't Nobodys Business*'. It was during their six month residency in Rome that they received letters from Jess Roden asking them to join him in a new band as he had just got a contract with Island. So as soon as they returned from Rome, Kevyn and Johnny teamed up with Jess. They then called on Robbie Blunt, and together with drummer Pete Robinson 'Bronco' was formed.

They soon all signed for Island and rehearsals began in earnest in Shatterford Village Hall. Later they had their own rehearsal rooms at Baynhams Farm in Trimpley, which Kevyn and Johnny had rented.

They were influenced by American West Coast groups like 'Buffalo Springfield', although they played with a harder edge. They wrote many of their own songs and had extra help from Cliff Ward on some numbers as well as playing songs such as 'Woodstock' by Joni Mitchell and 'Sweet Cocaine' by Laura Nyro. Live, they improvised, and extended some numbers to twenty minutes.

One of their first gigs was at Frank Freeman's in December 1969 and they were soon gigging extensively all over the country, thanks to their bookers Johnny Glover and Alec Leslie. These dates included the famous Roundhouse venue in Chalk Farm and also Glastonbury Festival in its early days. During their travels they often stayed at Steve Winwood's cottage in Berkshire.

They recorded their first album 'Country Home' at the Island Studios in Basing Street. They then had a series of successful gigs in Holland with 'Traffic' and 'Free' on an Island records package tour, appearing at clubs like the Milky Way and Paradiso in Amsterdam. They also had their first Radio One session in July 1970. After a heavy schedule of gigs and radio shows they eventually recorded their second album 'Ace Of Sunlight' in 1971. In the midst of all this continuing success, disaster struck. On their way home from a gig in Bristol they had serious crash on the M5 in May 1971. Both the roadies and Johnny Pasternak and Pete Robinson were seriously injured. This put them out of action for a few months and they lost momentum, which they never really regained.

In September they had to cancel a free concert they had arranged in Stourport to thank their fans, when they had to fly off to America for a

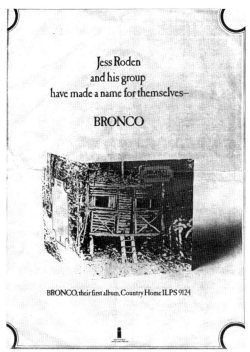

Flyer for Country Home Album

177

collection of gigs that had been set up for them. They were based in Los Angeles and stayed in a rather seedy motel on Sunset Strip called the Tropicana, but they were in good company as Tom Waits was a fellow guest there. They played at the Whisky-a-Go-Go for three nights, supporting blues star Freddy King. During their stay they became good friends with the promoter Mario who managed to get Robbie a stage-side view when the 'Allman Brothers' played there. It was not long after this that guitarist Duanne Allman was killed in a motorbike accident.

'Bronco' played in clubs all over California, San Francisco, Santa Barbara and Berkeley. When they played the famous surfers club, the Golden Bear in Huntington Beach, they met Ken Kesey and the 'Merry Pranksters' who were totally out of their heads on acid. They also nearly got arrested in Orange County when they failed to pull over for some traffic cops and were told in no uncertain terms that if they met them again they would be in serious trouble. After this warm and exotic month in the California sunshine, they returned to Kidderminster in November, and played a bonfire night charity gig on a freezing cold night in Mill Lane, Wolverley, to raise money to build a sports pavilion there. 'Bonehead' were also on the bill that night. Shortly after this Jess Roden and Robbie Blunt left the band. They made an album with Simon Kirk from 'Free' and keyboard player Rabbit Bundrick. Robbie then went on to join glam-rock band 'Silverhead', and later played with Robert Plant both here and in America. He is now a top session musician playing with people such as Phil Collins and Julian Lennon. Jess Roden sang on the 'Keef Hartley' album *Lancashire Hustler* in 1973. He then went to America in the same year and formed the 'Butts Band' with ex-'Doors' Robbie Krierger, guitar; John Densmore, drums and Phil Chen on bass. He was with Southampton band Iguana for a while and recorded several albums for Island. Elmer O'Shea joined the band on guitar

Somewhere in California l to r: Johnny Pasternak, Unknown friend, Robbie Blunt, Kevyn Gammond.

THE GOLDEN BEAR
306 OCEAN AVENUE (HWY 101)   HUNTINGTON BEACH

Golden Bear, Huntington Beach.

and Ron Tait on vocals, but Elmer didn't stay long and was replaced by Paul Lockey who played guitar and vocals. Ron Tait left shortly afterwards. They changed their record label to Polydor and a little later were joined by multi-instrumentalist Dan Fone who played everything from banjo and harmonica to keyboards. In August 1973 they released their third album *'Smoking Mixture'*. It was a little heavier and less country than before but it still contained a couple of Kevyn Gammond and Cliff Ward collaborations *'Attraction'* and *'Southbound Express'*. They also released a single with Cliff Ward's *'The Traveller'* on the B-side and a Gammond/Pasternak song, *'Steal That Gold'* on the A-side. They did the Kid Jensen Radio One show and also had good airplay on Radio Luxembourg and Radio London. By the end of 1973 the band split up. Despite everything they had done, the band never really lived up to its full potential, particularly Jess Roden, whose superb vocals should have brought him worldwide fame.

Kevyn Gammond eventually went on to become head of music at Kidderminster College, where he runs their own record label MAS Records. He also joined up with Robert Plant to play lead guitar in his 'Priory of Brion' group.

BRONCO – DISCOGRAPHY

LP'S
1970 *Country Home* – Island – ILPS 9124
1971 *Ace of Sunlight* – Island – ILPS 9161
1972 1973 – *Smoking Mixture* – Polydor 2383 215

SINGLES
Lazy Now/A Matter of Perspective – Chrysalis
wip 6096-1971
Steal that Gold/The Traveller - Polydor 2058 395 1973

ROBERT PLANT

Robert Plant was educated at Stourbridge Grammar School and later at Kidderminster College, although he spent a lot of time hanging around with the Stourbridge Art School crowd who were heavily into music and the beatnik scene of the time. One of his first groups was the totally forgotten 'Black Snake Moan', the drummer is thought to have been Rob Elcock. He then joined Kidderminster blues outfit the 'Crawling Kingsnakes', replacing Al King on vocals. While performing at Old Hill Plaza with the Kingsnakes, where he was also master of ceremonies, Robert was approached by John Bonham who said "You're not a bad singer, but the group needs another drummer", and recommended himself. When Robert found out he came from Redditch he said, "I don't care if you're Buddy Rich, I'm not picking you up from Redditch." Anyway Bonzo joined the band and along with Maverick, lead; Roy Price, rhythm, and Terry Edwards, bass, 'Crawling Kingsnakes' MK 2 was formed and they rehearsed in a hall in Clows Top. They played a lot locally and also the Ma Regan circuit around Birmingham.

Robert at Fillmore East, New York 1969
Photo Jeff Mayer

When they eventually split up he joined 'Listen' and recorded three singles for CBS and a couple of solo singles. It was at this time that Robert spoke of his love of obscure black soul and r'n'b artists such as Kris Kenner, Don Covay and OV Wright. When 'Listen' split up Robert formed the 'Band of Joy'. The first line up was from West Bromwich and the second from Wolverhampton. He finally teamed up with Kevyn Gammond on lead; Paul Lockey, bass; Chris Brown, keyboards, and John Bonham on drums, and 'Band of Joy' MK 3 was formed. They got on well together. With Kevyn's fiery avant-garde playing, Bonzo's explosive drumming and Robert's wailing vocals, the band really took off. They played at Frank Freeman's, a venue that Robert enjoyed because of its eclectic choice of acts from rock, blues and jazz to folk and even poetry, and he became friends with DJ's Paul Jennings and Rod Gilchrist. They played all over the country, thanks to their booker Barry Dickens of the Malcolm Rose Agency. They often gigged in Scotland and it was on their way there after a boozy gig at Exeter University, where Bonzo played the drums standing up, that Kevyn decided, after a row in the van, that enough was enough and got out of the van at Kidderminster. The band carried on to Scotland minus Kevyn. The lay-by outside Kevyn's house was familiar to Robert as he often slept in the van there, condensation dripping off the walls. Robert had fallen out with his parents at this time, who didn't think his choice of career was going to lead anywhere. Anyway with the absence of Kevyn, 'Band of Joy' MK 4 was formed with the addition of the Ball Brothers who had played with Ace Kefford, and guitarist Micky Strode. They had quite a few gigs with the likes of Terry Reid and Victor Brox and Robert was still a frequent visitor to Kidderminster, where he often called on Kevyn. In spite of all the work, money was in short

Robert Plant and John Bonham with Led Zeppelin somewhere in America. 1969 Photo: David Porter

supply and Robert often went laying tarmac to supplement his income. Eventually John Bonham got the drumming job with American singer/songwriter Tim Rose. He added a lot with his dynamic drumming on numbers like '*Morning Dew*', '*I Got a Loneliness*' and '*Come Away Melinda*'. John Bonham's departure spelled the end for the 'Band of Joy'.

Robert was on his own for a bit when he went to see Alexis Korner at the Cannon Hill Arts Centre. He was never slow in coming forward and asked Alexis if he could play harmonica in the second set. After a quick audition in the dressing room, which Robert passed with flying colours, he came on for the second half. He sang with Alexis Korner for some time before joining Walsall band 'Hobstweedle' whose main claim to fame was that their roadie was Noddy Holder's dad, who had a van which he used for window cleaning. It was whileRobert was rehearsing in the Three Men in a Boat pub in Walsall that he received a telegram from Peter Grant of RAK Music Management asking if he would like to join the 'Yardbirds'. Although he could hardly believe it, it turned out to be true. He was recommended by Terry Reid and shortly after Peter Grant turned up with Jimmy Page and Chris Dreja at Birmingham Teacher's Training College, where he was performing. Robert was chosen for the 'Yardbirds' and a new chapter in his life began.

He started off with the 'New Yardbirds' in June 1968 on £25 a week. He brought John Bonham with him and together with Jimmy Page on guitar and John Paul Jones on bass they formed the supergroup that became 'Led Zeppelin'. They played all the major clubs on the circuit such as the Marquee in Wardour Street and the Cherry Tree in Welwyn Garden City. I went myself to both those gigs and witnessed the mile-long queues that were forming outside the venues. They then went to Sweden and Denmark and returned as 'Led Zeppelin' in spite of protests by the Von Zeppelin family who didn't want their name to be associated with sex , drugs and rock 'n' roll. They flew off to America for the first time on December 23rd and arrived in Los Angeles on Christmas Eve, staying at the Continental Hyatt where they met up with old friend Terry Reid. They started off by opening up for Taj Mahal and 'Vanilla Fudge'. From there on everything went mad. They took off like wildfire, playing with'The Doors' in Seattle and then with just about everybody all over the country. They played a huge festival every weekend and Janis Joplin acted as a fairy godmother to Robert during this turbulent time. Within a year Robert had come from sleeping in a van in Kidderminster to playing a major part on the American rock scene. Instead of hearing about everything second-hand in England, here they were at the very heart of the American sub-culture. When they were in New York they often went to Steve Paul's Scene Club in Manhattan, where Jimi Hendrix used to jam with people like Jeff Beck, Tim Bogert on bass and Buddy Miles on drums, and where Debbie Harry was likely to walk in on the arms of some local mafia. The tables were always piled high with 'gear' on them. Over the next few years, they consolidated themselves in America, exploring and experimenting; the energy and electricity that surfaced for both Bonzo and Robert in 'Band of Joy ' just exploded in America. Sometimes, like at the Boston Tea Party, they played for four or five hours; there was no stopping them at this time.

It was a long way from Manhattan to Wolverley just north of Kidderminster but it was here in 1969 that Robert discovered a derelict old farmhouse that he decided to buy. It was in an amazing setting, but having been left for so many years, it was in a rough condition, ideal for stamping your own personality on it. So Robert went ahead and bought it. He knew the area well, having cycled there many times in his school and college days down the country lanes round the back of Kinver Edge to Wolverley. Here he relaxed and lived an entirely different life style, renovating his new home, playing tennis, occasional trips to Molineux to watch the Wolves, and visits to his local pub. Generally he preferred the quiet life to being a socialite, but remembers knocking around with Rod Stewart and playing games of football in his Hollywood mansion. During the 1970s 'Led Zeppelin' went on from success to success, but in 1980 John Bonham tragically died and the band finished.

Since then Robert has pursued many musical projects, as well as taking trips to India and North Africa, canoeing down the River Severn and being involved with various local charities.   All projects done with the same boundless energy and enthusiasm he has had since his early days with the 'Crawling Kingsnakes'.

'Band of Joy' recorded four numbers at Regent Sound Studios which were never released but were kept on acetate. Many years later Robert Plant included two tracks on the '*Sixty Six to Timbuktu*' double album, a stunning version of '*Hey Joe*' and a Stephen Stills song '*For What its Worth*'. Another song '*Adriatic Sea View*' was included on a compilation cassette '*In the Forest*' released by Kidderminster College under the guidance of Kevyn Gammond. Since then Kidderminster College, under their MAS record label have released a CD (MAS ATTACK 3) which includes 2 tracks featuring Robert Plant; '*Seaview* 'with 'The Band of Joy' and a version of '*Morning Dew*' with 'Priory of Brion'. 'Led Zeppelin's discography has been documented many times.

They have been the inspiration to thousands of groups and continue to do so to this day.

The Legend Lives On!

THE REFLECTIONS

1966 – 1982

Trevor Jones and Graham Drew had left Cliff Ward's 'Cruisers' after their return from France in the late summer of 1965, but by 1966 both Trevor and Graham were keen to get a new group going. They soon teamed up with Rodney Simmonds on rhythm; Paul McReath, drums, and Dave England, vocals, and called themselves 'The Reflections'. This line up lasted about six months when they mostly played covers and got plenty of work from the Mercian Agency, initially through their association with Cliff Ward's 'Cruisers'.

The Reflections 1968.
l to r Bruce Ward, Pete
Rowley, Trevor Jones,
Paul Mackreath, Graham
Drew, Roger Shapcott

In May 1967, Dave England was replaced on vocals by Bob Barber, and they added Roger Shapcote on sax and Abdul Benson on keyboards. This gave them a fuller sound and they started including a lot more sax numbers in their set like '*Stop Her On Sight*' by Edwin Starr and '*Knock on Wood*' by Eddie Floyd. They rehearsed at the Crown in Stourport where landlords Renee and Jock Bell had started a live music venue, 'Casa Fiesta'. Bob remembers well the luminous painted walls with bullfight scenes on them, watched with an attentive eye by landlady Renee. They played a few gigs there and also Stourport Civic where on one occasion they supported 'Wayne Fontana and the Mindbenders'. Other gigs followed in the area and around Birmingham, sometimes they were doing seven gigs a week. Their stage uniform changed from suits to kaftans as their sound got heavier and they changed their keyboard player first to Grant Balmer, then Pete Rowley and then Alan Brooks. Always on the lookout for numbers to record, they were given a song *'Cartagena'*, written by Cliff Ward after a trip he had made to Spain. He took the recording himself to Island Records but nothing more was heard of it.

Early in 1969, after a gig in Wolverhampton supporting American soul singer Mary Wells, Bob Barber left the band. He was replaced on vocals by Bob Ward. With changes in line up the band carried on until 1982.. Graham Drew left to join the 'Association Show Band'. Always a versatile and hardworking group 'The Reflections' were one of the most popular bands of that era.

Sadly, Graham Drew died at the age of 58 in March 2002.

SLAMHAMMER

1968 - 1971

Martyn Price and Trevor Scragg were good friends at Dudley Tech in 1967, and like many young men of that time became very keen on 'the blues'; people like BB King, John Mayall and Eric Clapton. With Martyn on drums and Trevor on guitar they got in Barry Southall to learn the bass. Initially they had folk singer Nick Powell on vocals, but his image didn't quite fit. They then met Dave Deakin who had the image; green shoes, yellow laces and a purple jacket; always rolling a joint. Although Dave's image was fine, his vocals didn't quite fit either. One night outside the Wharf, they heard this great harmonica player. They went to check him out. He had the right look and could sing as well, so Martin Lee from Stourport became their new vocalist. This was in 1968 and with a regular line up they started gigging with support spots at the Wharf to bands like 'Free' and 'Yes'. Somewhere they spotted pianist John Bates and he joined the group. The only trouble was that pianos at venues in those days were abysmal, so John got himself a Hammond organ. With a slightly more progressive sound they got plenty more gigs supporting 'Black Sabbath', 'Jethro Tull', and Joe Cocker at the Black Horse, when he was number one in the charts. When they got a call to play Mothers in Birmingham, they were determined to play this prestige venue, the only problem was that Martyn and his drum kit were on the wrong side of the River Severn. So with desperate calls to the ferryman at Arley, they persuaded him to cross Martyn and the drum kit over to the Kidderminster side of the river where the band were waiting with the van and on they went to Mothers. The main band that night, 'Curved Air', failed to turn up.

In 1970 newly formed band 'Bonehead' pinched Martin Lee from them and they got a new singer Dave from Bristol. At this time Trevor started introducing his own songs and taking the band in a new direction. This led to friction with John Bateswho left in 1971. They carried on for another six months their last gig supporting 'The Kinks' at the Top Rank in Birmingham. That was the end of 'Slamhammer'. Martyn Price moved to Ludlow, and these days he plays bass and makes leather clothes and goods. John Bates currently plays with 'Curtis Little and the Receivers' and he is also a journalist and lecturer in Music Technology at Kidderminster College.

CLIFFORD T. WARD

The beginning of 1968 saw Cliff studying hard at Worcester Teacher Training College, although he hadn't given up his musical interests. He had been demo-ing his new single for CBS '*Naughty Boy*' with the help of Ken Wright and Bev Pegg. Unbeknown to Ken, he even formed another 'Simons Secrets' which was the old 'Bridge St Jump Band', including Ian Simmonds on guitar and Rob Elcock on drums. The single was released in April, followed by a second single '*Keeping My Head Above Water*', which was released at the end of the year. Neither record did very much and the year brought to an end the many incarnations of Cliffs beat groups.

Photo: Friends of Clifford T Ward

Undeterred, Cliff kept on making demos at Bev's studio in Kinver and in autumn 1970 took up a full time teaching post at Bromsgrove High School. Cliff still had a publishing contract with Blue Mountain Music and was writing songs for 'Bronco' with Kevyn Gammond including '*A Matter Of Perspective*', B-side of a single, and '*Misfit On Your Stair*', on their '*Country Home*' album. Meanwhile, loyal and helpful friend Ken Wright had moved to London and got a job as an accountant at the BBC. He passed one of Cliff's tapes on to John Peel's producer, John Walters, who in turn passed it on to Clive Selwood, former head of Electra Records in the UK, who had formed Dandelion Records with John Peel in October 1971. They started the label to promote new artists and Clive was particularly keen on Cliff's songs. So Cliff became Dandelion's latest signing, under the signature of Clifford T Ward.

They started recording almost straight away at the Marquee studios in London in January 1972, and got in Richard Hewson to do the string

187

Cliff at work at the Chipping Norton studio
Photo: Friends of Clifford T Ward

arrangement. Richard had worked with James Taylor and the Beatles, so he had quite a pedigree. The album was called *'Singer-Songwriter'* and was launched with a small promotional gig at the Speakeasy with Derek Thomas, Kevyn Gammond and Johnny Pasternak in the backing group. In spite of heavy publicity and Radio One shows like Johnny Walker and Sounds of the 70s, the two singles released, *'Carrie'* and then *'Coathanger'* did not generate large sales. Even so Clive Selwood's enthusiasm was undiminished and Cliff's second album was half-recorded when Clive and John Peel decided to close down Dandelion Records. Clive Selwood managed to place Cliff with Charisma Records, and so in January 1973, Cliff found himself on a major label with half an album already completed.

After listening to a demo of *'Home Thoughts'* the second album's title, Tony Stratton-Smith the owner of Charisma Records was enthusiastic about Cliff's "Pure English voice" and was right behind the record. Recording continued with Derek Thomas on guitar. Derek, who was a reporter on the Kidderminster Shuttle, had been with Cliff for some time, was joined by ex-'Crawling Kingsnakes' and 'Bonehead' bassist Terry Edwards. Ken Wright was on drums and Richard Hewson came in again for the string arrangement. They did another John Peel radio session where they played *'Gaye'* and other tracks off the forthcoming album. The recording was finished in February, and after various remixes and a recutting, *'Home Thoughts'* was eventually released in April 1973, to ecstatic reviews in the music press. The single *'Gaye'* was released first and was slow to move, but with extensive playing and nationwide publicity, using the schoolteacher angle, it reached the Top 50 in June, eventually rising to number eight.

Although never a huge hit *'Home Thoughts'* is a classic album and has sold well over many years. All this success brought an abrupt end to Cliff's teaching career and he gave his notice in to Bromsgrove High School.

The media circus began for Cliff with rounds of radio and TV spots including two appearances on Top of the Pops. He was not so keen on live performances and only had one high profile gig at the Queen Elizabeth Hall in London, where he appeared supportingTwiggy. *'Gaye'* was even a number five later in Brazil, but was never materialised on. The musicians on the album, Derek Thomas, Ken Wright and Terry Edwards, all went on to successful careers in their various ways. As for Cliff, all those years of one night stands and countless hours of songwriting and recording had finally paid off and he had an interesting career ahead of him, until he was struck down by multiple sclerosis in the mid-80s which led to a premature death in 2001. But we leave Cliff in 1973 enjoying well-deserved success with *'Home Thoughts'*, written and sung by Clifford T. Ward.

DISCOGRAPHY

1968 – 1973 – up to Home Thoughts

Singles

'Naughty Boy/Sympathy' – Simon's Secrets on CBS
April 1968

'Keeping My Head Above Water/I Know What Her Name Is'. Simon's Secrets on CBS
December 1968

'Carrie/Sidetrack' – Clifford T. Ward on Dandelion -
August 1972

'Coathanger/Rayne' Clifford T. Ward on Charisma –
October 1972.

'Gaye/Home Thoughts From Abroad' – Clifford T. Ward
on Charisma
April 1973

LP's

'Singer-Songwriter' on Dandelion - August 1972

'Home Thoughts' on Charisma - April 1973

WISE VIRGIN

Wise Virgin were formed in the late autumn of 1968. Prime mover was keyboard player Abdul Benson, previously with 'The Reflections' and 'Custard Tree'. Abdul was working at the Kidderminster Shuttle at the time, and got in reporter Derek Thomas to join on guitar. Ex-'Custard Tree' bass player George Kristic also joined, together with Dave Bodley on drums and Robin Walker, a strong vocalist in the style of Joe Cocker. Rehearsals began in an old nissen hut in Stourport. The band played underground material from the likes of 'Steppenwolf' and 'Velvet Underground'. They went out on the road in December 1968. One of their first gigs was at Kidderminster College where they played with 'The Action' and Kevyn Gammond's 'Mad Dog'. Plenty of gigs followed including support spots at Malvern Winter Gardens thanks to Norman Dickens. They also acquired a manager, David Virr, who had contacts through his work as a DJ. David had also been vocalist in Stourbridge r'n'b band 'The Puritans'. His main claim to fame was that he sang on stage with Robert Plant in one of his early groups 'Black Snake Moan'. 'Wise Virgin' played at Oxford when Richard Branson turned up. Did the name attract him? George left and was replaced on bass by Terry Edwards.

The band split up towards the end of 1969, and Derek Thomas and Terry Edwards went to play with Clifford T. Ward on his *Home Thoughts* album. Abdul Benson formed progressive rock group 'Salamander' whose album, *The Ten Commandments*' has become quite a collector's item. George Kristic got married and stayed out of music for quite a few years, until he bought the Rook studios in Stourport from Roy Robbins, which he renamed Saxon Studios. Dave Bodley joined 'Love's Playground', a covers band who played mostly soul numbers. Other members included ex-Custard Tree', Mick Casey, Lyn and harmonica player Mad John, and guitarist/vocalist Bobby Poole, who sadly died of leukaemia a few years later. 'Love's Playground' had loads of gigs but eventually split up in March 1970.

PEOPLE AND EVENTS
1968 - 1972

1968 was a vintage year for rock and pop in Kidderminster. Frank Freeman began his progressive rock gigs. The Wharf, the Chateau and the Black Horse also regularly put on top bands. All this activity was reported in the Kidderminster Shuttle by Malcolm Nicholl, in his 'On The Inside' column.

1965

Sunday 7th January

> The new year started off with a bang when Frank Freeman's had drummer Aynsley Dunbar Retaliation on his Sunday night rock club. Victor Brox was on vocals. Chris Farlow appeared at the Chateau.

Friday 19th January

> 'The Indigo Set' announced they were to split up at the end of the month.

Sunday 21st January

> Peter Green's 'Fleetwood Mac' made a sensational appearance at Frank Freeman's with guest American bluesman Eddie Boyd on vocals.

Sunday 11th February

> Chicken Shack appeared at Frank Freeman's, while the previous weekend Graham Bond was at the Chateau. They also played the College Dance at the Town Hall the following Saturday.

Sunday 18th Febraury

> American singing star Tim Rose made a controversial appearance at Franks. The singer of '*Morning Dew*' made few concessions to the audience, definitely no encores!

Jeremy Spenser and Mick
Fleetwood at Frank
Freeman's January 21st
1968
Photos Colin Hill

Simon Nicoll & Judy
Dyble of Fairport
Convention at Frank
Freemans March 24th 1968
Photo Colin Hill

Chicken Shack
l to r Dave Bidwell &
Stan Webb
Photo Colin Hill

Christine Perfect
Photo Colin Hill

192

Sunday 3rd Mar ch

Guitarist Jet Harris was interviewed at the Wharf where Billie Davies was appearing. On the previous night 'Ten Years After' played at the Chateau.

Friday 15th March

New Stourport group 'The Breakdown' had just been formed. Visiting Frank's on Sunday were Marquee regulars 'The Gods' with Greg Lake on bass.

Sunday 24th March

'Fairport Convention' appeared at Frank's to tie in with the release of their new single *'She Wears a Ribbon Bow'*. A competition was held to find the girl with the prettiest bow. One of the judges was Judy Dyble from the group. The winner was Jacqueline Legierski of Chester Road North. In the same week 'Tommy and the Crestas' introduced a new line up with Dave Poutney on organ and Roger Mason on bass.

Friday 5th April

Cliff Ward released a new single *'Naughty Boy'* on the CBS label. His group is now called 'Simons Secrets'. The line up is Cliff on vocals; Dave Holder, bass; Rob Elcock , drums; Dave Conway, rhythm, and Ian Simmons, lead guitar.

Sunday 14th April

There was an 'all-niter' at Frank's on Easter Sunday. Headlining were 'Tyrannosaurus Rex' with Marc Bolan and Peregrine Took, who came on stage about 3 o'clock on Monday morning. Also on the bill were 'Doctor K's Blues Band' and 'Junior Eyes'. On the previous Thursday 'Blossom Toes' headlined the student's dance at Kidderminster College.

Sunday 12th May

Top group 'Spooky Tooth' appeared at Frank's on Sunday.

Monday 13th May

Kidderminster Playhouse staged its last play this week. *Gloriana*, written by nonentities chairman Kenneth Rose, was a play with music about the life of Queen Elizabeth I. This was to be the last performance at the Playhouse.

Tyrannosaurus Rex at
Frank Freemans April 14th
1968
Photo Colin Hill

Sunday 19th May

'Captain Beefheart' made his legendary appearance at Frank's this Sunday. John Peel was there to record some of the numbers for posterity. The band were pleased with their reception although their amplification gave them some trouble. "Very nice" said John Peel. Both he and 'Captain Beefheart' were impressed by the club in such a small town. On the same night Chris Farlow and 'The Thunderbirds' appeared at the Wharf.

Friday 21st June

Frank Freeman announced that the Sunday Club was to close until August, as it was difficult to book the top groups during the summer season. Local singer Peter Wynne, now known as Simon Smith, won an appearance on 'Opportunity Knocks'. He would eventually appear in the European Song Contest at Knokke in Belgium.

Friday 28th June

The 'Brian Auger Trinity' with Julie Driscoll on vocals got rave reviews for their appearance at the college dance at Stourport Civic. So did Joe Cocker who with his 'Grease Band' played the Wharf on Sunday night.

Captain Beefheart with
his Magic Band and John
Peel at Frank Freeman's
May 19th 1968
Photo Colin Hill

Friday 19th July

Local group 'Liquorice' made their debut appearance at the home of Charles Talbot in a charity gig. The rock trio were Robbie Blunt, lead guitar; John Pasternak, bass and Dave Bodley on drums.

1st/2nd September

'The Bluesology Festival' at the Chateau was spoilt by rainy weather.
(Sun/Mon)

This two day festival was plagued by heavy showers but it did not stop a range of top groups appearing. Hosted by Radio One DJ John Peel, the bands included Peter Green's 'Fleetwood Mac' with new guitarist Danny Kirwan, John Mayalls 'Bluesbreakers', Geno Washington, Joe Cocker and his 'Grease Band', 'The Family', 'Wynder K. Frogg', 'The Move' and 'Skip Bifferty'.

Friday20th September

Local football hero Alun Evans, was transferred from Wolves to Liverpool and kept £5,000 for himself; a lot of money in those days.

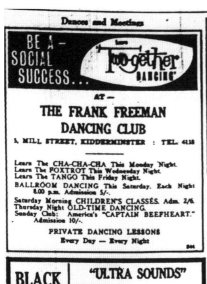
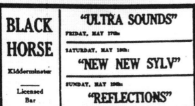
Tuesday 1st October
'Skip Bifferty' appeared at the Black Horse. This entertaining band had already made a successful appearance at Frank Freeman's. It was announced this week that local group 'Custard Tree' would split up this month due to internal frictions.

Sunday 6th October
Frank Freeman's club started again this Sunday with top group 'Tea and Symphony'. Also on the bill was folk singer Jo-Anne Kelly and with John Peel as DJ, the new sessions got off to a flying start. 'Liquorice' announced that they had a new drummer Richard 'Mooney' Marzola, ex-'Rubber Duck' from Worcester.

Sunday 13th Oct ober
Gordon Smith and Tim Houllier played blues and folk at Frank's this Sunday, also on the bill was local rock trio 'Liquorice'.

Friday 14th October
'The Peddlers' appeared at the Black Horse this week. The trio, with jazz influences, played to a packed house. They were one of promoter Norman Dicken's favourite groups.

Sunday 20th October
'Eclection' played at Frank Freeman's.

Sunday 1st September

TIMES	ARTISTS
12.00 a.m. — 12.45 p.m.	Disc Jockey
12.45 p.m. — 1.45 p.m.	Jasper Stubbs and His GloryLand Band
1.55 p.m. — 2.25 p.m.	Duster Bennett
2.35 p.m. — 3.05 p.m.	John Mayall's Bluesbrakers
3.10 p.m. — 3.40 p.m.	Duster Bennett
3.50 p.m. — 4.35 p.m.	Cliff Bennett
4.45 p.m. — 5.45 p.m.	Jasper Stubbs and His GloryLand Band
5.55 p.m. — 6.25 p.m.	John Mayall's Bluesbrakers
6.25 p.m. — 7.00 p.m.	Disc Jockey
7.00 p.m. — 7.15 p.m.	John Peel — Radio One Disc Jockey
7.15 p.m. — 8.00 p.m.	Cliff Bennett
8.10 p.m. — 8.55 p.m.	Geno Washington and The Ram Jam Band
9.05 p.m. — 9.50 p.m.	Jo Cocker
10.00 p.m. — 11.00 p.m.	The Passion Forest
11.10 p.m. — 11.55 p.m.	Geno Washington and The Ram Jam Band
12.05 a.m. — 12.55 a.m.	Jo Cocker
1.10 a.m. — 2.10 a.m.	The Passion Forest

Monday 2nd September

TIMES	ARTISTS
11.00 a.m. — 12.00 p.m.	Group Competition
12.00 p.m. — 12.45 p.m.	Radio One Disc Jockey — John Peel
12.45 p.m. — 1.45 p.m.	The Breakthru'
1.55 p.m. — 2.25 p.m.	Chris Farlowe, with Wynder K. Frogg
2.45 p.m. — 3.20 p.m.	The Move
3.30 p.m. — 4.30 p.m.	The Breakthru'
4.40 p.m. — 5.10 p.m.	Fleetwood Mac
5.20 p.m. — 5.50 p.m.	Chris Farlowe with Wynder K. Frogg
6.00 p.m. — 6.35 p.m.	The Move
6.45 p.m. — 7.15 p.m.	Fleetwood Mac
7.25 p.m. — 8.10 p.m.	Skip Bifferty
8.20 p.m. — 9.05 p.m.	The Family
9.15 p.m. — 10.15 p.m.	The Freddie Mack Show
10.25 p.m. — 11.25 p.m.	Rebellion
11.35 p.m. — 12.20 a.m.	The Family
12.30 a.m. — 1.30 a.m.	The Freddie Mack Show

Tuesday 22nd October

Jess Roden appeared at the Black Horse with 'The Alan Bown Set'.

Thursday 24th Oct ober

The Swan Centre was opened today. The project cost £1,000,000 and was opened by the Mayor, Councillor Micklewright. This development replaced the heart of old Kidderminster.

Friday 25th October

Richard Matthews had an interview with John Peel in the 'On the Inside' column, in which he praised Frank Freemans club for having such a progressive music scene.

Sunday 27th October

Five acts appeared at Frank's this Sunday including one- man band Duster Bennet. Kevyn Gammond introduced his new group 'Mad

Dog' for an half hour's "Muck about" playing progressive rock with jazz influences. Also on the bill were poet and humorist Ron Geesin, folk singer Jack Gibson and local blues outfit 'Slamhammer'. On Tuesday 29th 'Spooky Tooth' appeared at the Black Horse.

Sunday 3rd November

'Barclay James Harvest' impressed a full house at Frank's with their progressive music which featured a melotron. Also appearing that night was Radio One DJ Pete Drummond. While on Tuesday 'Spooky Tooth' played to a full house at the Black Horse.

Sunday 10th November

'Pete Browns Battered Ornaments' played at Frank's this Sunday. They were a very original band with Pete Brown quoting poetry and playing the trumpet, as well as singing. They did not draw a very big crowd, maybe because 'Chicken Shack' were playing at the Wharf the same night.

Tuesday 12th November

Joe Cocker together with his 'Grease Band' gave a stunning performance at the Black Horse. His record '*With A Little Help From My Friends*' was number one in the charts, and the Black Horse was naturally packed to the rafters. Joe Cocker enjoyed the gig and wanted to make a return visit.

Sunday 17th November

'Jethro Tull' made an impressive first appearance at the Wharf, particularly their front man Ian Anderson. While 'Love Sculpture' appeared at Frank's with their hit record '*Sabre Dance*'.

Tues day 19th November

'Wynder K. Frogg', the organist, headlined at the Black Horse this Tuesday. Since Jimmy Cliff's disappearance, Wynder K. Frogg had taken over the leadership of his group, which included former John Mayall saxophonist Chris Mercer.

Wednesday 20th November

Harriers lost their FA cup replay 1-0 to Brighton at Aggborough. There was a record-breaking crowd of 8,442.

Friday 22nd November

Frank Freeman's got an article written in the underground newspaper 'The International Times'. It recommended its readers to visit the club in Kidderminster.

Sunday 24th November

'Principal Edwards Magic Theatre' appeared at Frank's this Sunday. They provided a fantasy show of singing, dancing and lighting with guitar, bass, drums, violin and flute. Also on the bill was sitar player Vidas Serelis.

Sunday 1st December

Underground group 'Junior Eyes' appeared at Frank's.

Tuesday 10th December

'The Savoy Brown Blues Band' appeared at the Black Horse. Also this week Cliff Ward's new group, now called 'Simon's Secrets' released a new single called '*I Know What Her Name Is*'.

Monday 16th December

'Chicken Shack' were the star attraction at the Briars on Monday night at a gig to raise money for the Youth Centre Fund, organised by Cllr. Charles Talbot.

Sunday 22nd December

'Eclection' were at Frank's on Sunday with a new single '*Please*', and a new singer, Doris Henderson. Local group 'Bartholomew's Creed' announced a new lead guitarist, Elmer O'Shea.

1969

1969 was another busy year in Kidderminster. Two sex symbols of the sixties were on the film screens the first week of January. Marianne Faithful starred in 'Girl on a Motorbike' at the Haven in Stourport, while Julie Christie was in Thomas Hardy's 'Far from the Madding Crowd' at the ABC. The classic film 'The Graduate' with Dustin Hoffman and Anne Bancroft was on at the ABC the following week.

Sunday 12th January

'Blonde on Blonde' appeared at Frank's this Sunday. At the cinema Sean Connery and Brigitte Bardot appeared in the western 'Shalako' at the ABC.

Friday 17th January

Three groups appeared at the college dance this Friday. 'The Action' from London had a West Coast Sound. Kevyn Gammond impressed with his guitar playing in his new group 'Mad Dog', while another new Kidderminster group 'Wise Virgin' also appeared.

Sunday 19th January

'The Third Ear Band' appeared at Frank's where they played acoustically with a violin, cello, oboe and bongo drums. Back by popular request at Frank's are 'Junior Eyes', while another very popular group 'Spooky Tooth' made their second appearance at the Black Horse on Tuesday the 21st. Also on Sunday 'The Free' are playing at the Wharf.

Sunday 26th January

Ex-members of Custard Tree joined together to form new group 'Love's Playground'. They play the Wharf this Sunday.

Friday 31st January

Demolition work continues in earnest in the redevelopment of the town, including Josiah Stallard and Sons and the George Inn, both at the end of Mill Street. Kidderminster Playhouse was finally razed to the ground to make way for the ring road. At the Wharf three ex-'Traffic' members, Jim Capaldi, Chris Wood and Dave Mason joined

'Wynder K. Frogg' for an impromptu set.

Sunday 9th February

Anarcho rockers the 'Edgar Broughton Band' appeared at Frank's, also on the bill was blues singer Gordon Smith.

Sunday 16th February

'Eclection' made their third appearance at Frank's this Sunday. This popular and exciting group will soon embark on a six week tour of America and Canada.

Sunday 23rd February

London group 'Van Der Graaf Generator' played at Frank's this Sunday, while 'Red Beans and Rice' appeared at the Wharf. 'Chicken Shack' guitarist Stan Webb married Lyn Silvester, bass guitarist Andy's sister, at Broome Church. As well as members of 'Chicken Shack', some of 'Fleetwood Mac' and 'Slamhammer' were in the congregation.

Sunday 2nd March

One-man blues band Duster Bennett appeared at Frank's.

Wednesday 5th March

There was a sit down concert at the college this Wednesday with the stage in the centre of the hall. It was a double bill featuring 'The Strawbs' and Roy Harper, which turned out to be a successful format.

Sunday 9th March

Spoilt for choice again on a Sunday with 'Yes' making their first appearance at Frank's. They were regulars at the Marquee in London and had just appeared with 'Cream' at their farewell concert at the Albert Hall. At the Wharf, drummer Keef Hartley headlined with his own band, previously having played with John Mayalls 'Bluesbreakers'.

Sunday 16th March

'Junior Eyes' made a welcome return to Frank's, their hard driving rock makes them one of the most popular groups there.

Friday 28th March

Birmingham group 'Idle Race' played at the College Rag Dance. Lead by Jeff Lynne, the 'Idle Race' were one of the most promising new groups of 1969. The College Rag Week had an unusual twist in this year when the Rag Queen turned out to be a boy. Eighteen year old Chris Marcus entered for a joke and won the competition. At the Park Attwood go-go dancer Tina appeared with the Dave Munro Disco.

Sunday 27th April

'Caravan' appeared at Franks. Local drummer Sean Jenkins appeared with his group 'Elastic Band' playing their own compositions on BBC TV's *Colour Me Pop*.

Sunday 11th May

'Yes' received rave reviews for their exciting appearance at Frank's this Sunday.

Sunday 18th May

'Spirit of John Morgan' appeared at Frank's, having just returned from a tour of France with Memphis Slim and John Lee Hooker.

Sunday 8th June

Exciting new group 'King Crimson' appeared at Frank's, while the 'Savoy Brown Blues Band' were at the Wharf.

Friday 13th June

'Chicken Shack' were on Top of the Pops this week as their latest single *'I'd Rather Go Blind'* entered the charts at number 17. Kidderminster vocalist Jess Roden, who sings with Alan Bown, released a single last week entitled *'Still As Stone'*. They were hoping for a hit this time after several near misses.

Sunday 7th September

'Earth' who later became 'Black Sabbath' headlined at the Wharf, supported by 'Deaf Cuckoo' with Elmer O'Shea on guitar.

Sunday 14th September

Frank's re-opened after the summer break with singer Bridget St John who recorded on John Peel's Dandelion label. Also on the bill were two man outfit 'Blondel' who played twelve instruments between them.

Monday 15th Sept ember

Clee Hall Country Club was raided by the police at midnight. Scores of young people were dancing to ear- splitting music from disc jockey Dave Munro.

Sunday 21st September

'Yes' made their fourth appearance at Frank's with a superb performance to a full capacity crowd; support were local band 'Deaf Cuckoo'.

Sunday 6th October

Blues group 'The Groundhogs' played Frank's this Sunday. While this weekend local group 'Deaf Cuckoo' acquired a new member, vocalist 'Butch' Humber.

Sunday 7th December

'Chicken Shack' had a great performance at Frank's. One of the best blues groups in the country, lead guitarist Stan Webb was on top form, leaping about and cracking jokes with the audience.

Friday 12th December

Ralph McTell put in a superb performance at the Mare and Colt folk club.

Sunday 14th December

Jess Roden had left the 'Alan Bown Set' and teamed up with Kevyn Gammond to form new group 'Bronco' who played their second gig at Frank's this Sunday. Also in the band were Johnny Pasternak, bass; Robbie Blunt, guitar, and Pete Robinson, drums. Their music ranged from jazz to blues and country with Jess Roden on vocals in fine form.

Monday 15th December

The ever popular 'Junior Eyes' headline at Stourport Civic with 'Deaf Cuckoo' as support.

Sunday 21st December

American group 'Daddy Longlegs' appeared at Frank's.

1970

The new decade carried on the same as the old with plenty of live music to choose from.

Sunday 11th January

'Galliard' opened up at Franks with support from 'Deaf Cuckoo'. 'Galliard' got a good review; their music was described as jazz/rock with folk and blues influences. Birmingham heavy rock band 'Black Sabbath' were billed for the following Sunday with a certain Ozzy Osbourne on vocals. At the other extreme Frank Freeman had a programme of big bands on at Stourport Civic Centre with Joe Loss on Monday June 14th and Victor Sylvester playing on Valentine's night.

Friday 6th February

Owners of Clee Hall Country Club in Cookley were fined £506 for serving late drinks to non-members after hours, when there was no live music or food provided, only a discotheque available for entertainment.

Friday 10th April

Stourport had a rare visit from the circus when Sir Robert Fossett put up his big top at Severn Meadows. Featured were lions, tigers and a group of baby elephants, as well as the usual clowns etc.

Thursday 14th May

'Principal Edwards Magic Theatre' appeared at Kidderminster Town Hall. Also on the bill were 'Ket's Rebellion' and 'Probe'.

Monday 22nd June

The second stage of Kidderminster ring road was opened today. The section stretched from Coventry Street to Station Hill.

Thursday 18th June

'Bronco' played well to a small audience at Kidderminster College and Jess Roden's vocals were praised as usual. At the Haven cinema Stourport, Maggie Smith starred in the film *'The Prime of Miss Jean Brodie'*.

Wednesday 29th July

'Chicken Shack' left for a tour of America. Their LP *'Accept'* is riding high in Europe. They are as popular as ever in spite of the departure of Christine Perfect. She was replaced by Paul Raymond on keyboards.

Saturday 1st August

After a successful tour of Holland, 'Bronco' played Kidderminster Town Hall. Once again they had a good write up and played quite a few numbers off their forthcoming Island LP. On Sunday 'Bonehead' made their debut at the Wharf. The line up was Martin Lee, vocals (ex-'Slamhammer'); Elmer O'Shea, lead guitar (ex-'Deaf Cuckoo'); Terry Edwards, bass (ex-'Crawling Kingsnakes') and Colin Hawkins, drums (ex-'Mad Dog').

Friday 14th August

Frank Freeman announces that he hopes to start up the Sunday club again offering afternoon concerts, with the emphasis on acoustic sets rather than heavy rock, and also some folk and jazz evenings, if the demand is there.

Friday 23rd October

Hartlebury Village Hall was set to become a pop venue featuring top bands. First up was chart group 'White Plains'.

Sunday 4th October

Frank Freeman started off his Sunday afternoon concerts with folk/rock group 'The Strawbs'. This was quite a scoop for the club as 'The Strawbs' were making a breakthrough all over the country.

Friday 6th November

Kidderminster's £85,000 hole in the ground was near completion. The sunken traffic island at the junction of Comberton Hill and the ring road was due to be finished this week. The sunken island, which measures 178 x 172 feet, includes the site of the old Playhouse.

Friday 13th November

Pop promoters Peter Phillips and Nigel Rees were reported to be looking for new premises after the closure of the dances at the Park Atwood after six very successful years.

Saturday 21st November

Top pop group 'Edison Lighthouse' will appear at the Hartlebury Village Hall. They had a number one hit with *'Love Grows Where My Rosemary Goes'*. Popular local group 'The Crestas' will play support.

Sunday 24th November

'The Strawbs' made a welcome return to Frank's. They played to a packed house and had a tremendous reception with two encores. Highlights were Dave Cousin's lyrics and an outstanding organ performance from Rick Wakeman. Sixteen year old Vicky Littleton was particularly impressed. She was sitting cross-legged on the floor during the interval when Richard Hudson's sitar fell on her head and rearranged her hair which she had just straightened with an iron on brown paper. No serious damage was done.

Friday 4th December

Malcolm Nicholl, news editor of the Shuttle was named 'News reporter of the year'. He was chosen for the work he did for the Shuttle in 1969, which included his excellent reporting of the music scene, particularly at Frank Freeman's.

Sunday 6th December

'Tea and Symphony' made an impressive appearance at Franks with a theatrical performance which included mime, lighting and visual effects and also a very accomplished rock and acoustic set. Support band on the night were 'The Dog that Bit People'.

Sunday 13th December

One-man blues band Duster Bennett appeared at Frank's on Sunday. His LP *'12 Db's'* is selling well at the moment. Local group 'Bonehead' are support band, with new guitarist and singer Paul Lockey.

Wednesday 16th December

Three popular local groups, 'The Crestas', 'Reflections' and 'Breakdown' joined forces for a Christmas dance at Stourport Civic.

While at Stone Manor, top comedian Frankie Howerd appeared in cabaret, where he opened the new banqueting hall.

Sunday 20th December

'Barclay James Harvest' appeared at Frank's this Sunday. Only a three-piece group they were augmented by a mellotron, which produced some beautiful string effects, making them sound like a full orchestra. Despite some technical problems they turned in an excellent performance. Support on the night were local group 'Slammhammer'.

Sunday 27th December

Frank Freeman held his Boxing Day party with an afternoon concert at the club. A very confident 'Bronco' entertained the capacity crowd with fine performances from dual lead guitarists Kev Gammond and Robbie Blunt, and superb vocals from Jess Roden, in spite of his raging toothache. It was their first home town appearance since the release of their *Country Home* LP. After 'Bronco' there was a rare opportunity to 'see 'Led Zeppelin front man Robert Plant on stage, where he also played the guitar. It was something of a lower profile the following afternoon when 'Salamander' took the stage with Abdul Benson on mellotron. They were supported by folk artist Ian Highfield who played contemporary folk from the likes of Bob Dylan, James Taylor and Leonard Cohen.

1971

1971 saw the beginning of the end of 'the sixties'; the number of live music venues grew less during the year, apart from a series of soul gigs at Stourport Civic.

Sunday 10th January

Frank Freeman announced that Scunthorpe group 'Ka' would be the last band to appear at this legendary venue. Higher band fees and falling attendances finally put paid to the Sunday club. As Frank himself said, "It seems I'm flogging a dead horse". In fact there were a few more gigs before they finally finished. There was also trouble at the Black Horse where Nigel Mills began Thursday nights as 'Over 21 sessions', with more cabaret than rock, probably due to the large numbers of fights which were happening at the time.

Sunday 17th February

Omar Sharif, Julie Christie and Geraldine Chaplin starred in the famous film '*Doctor Zhivago*' at the ABC for seven days.

Saturday 20th February

'Fairweather', formerly 'Amen Corner', appeared at Stourport Civic, also on the bill were Jamaican band 'Frankie and the Countdowns'.

Saturday 6th March

Hit band 'The Equals' ('*Baby Come Back*') appear at Stourport Civic supported by Hereford group 'Woodfall'.

Friday 19th March

Radio One DJ Emperor Rosko appeared at Stourport Civic. The following Friday 'Jimmy James and the Vagabonds' were there. The next Saturday 'Johnny Johnson and the Bandwagon' were at the Civic.

Saturday 1st May

'Bronco' had a serious accident when their van crashed on the M5 returning home from a gig in Bristol. Pete Robinson had head injuries and was unconscious. Also badly hurt were bassist Johnny Pasternak and roadies Dick Haynes and Alan Stone.

Saturday 8th May

Stourport Civic Centre held a 'Hottest Hot Pants' competition. Dozens of 'delectable dollies' turned up on the night. The winner was Shirley Horton from Droitwich.

Thursday 13th May

Radio One Club visited Stourport Civic, with DJ Noel Edmunds. The show included an interview with Birmingham singer Raymond Frogatt. Hundreds of teenage fans turned up.

Friday 14th May

It was announced that Worcester Cross Youth Club was to close after twenty-five years. The pre-fab temporary building was initially the War Workers Club. It was turned into a youth club in 1946 when the war ended. Many groups in the 50s and 60s started off here. Later it was home to the Irish Club which housed rock and punk bands in the late 1970s.

Saturday 15th May
American girl group 'The Flirtations' appeared at Stourport Civic.

Friday 18th June
The Shuttle featured an article on twenty-year-old Nigel Pheysey who had just got a job as the Lord Mayor's Chauffeur. He had previously been 'Bronco's roadie, but now he had swapped his long hair, jeans and kaftan for a hair cut and suit to go with the new job.

Friday 23rd July
The Shuttle had an article by Derek Thomas about Arch Hill Square. This picturesque area of Kidderminster is now demolished and all that remains are the cobbles and blue bricks of the old pathway, which the conservationists were trying hard to save.

Wednesday 1st Sept   ember
A new £115,000 youth club centre was opened in Bromsgrove Street. Six years of hard work on fund raising for the new building, was carried out by Alderman Charles Talbot, who started when he was Mayor. It replaces the old Worcester Cross Youth Club, which closed in May. Two hundred youngsters turned up to dance to disco music and use the tennis tables, dartboard and badminton courts.

Saturday 11th September
'Bronco' cancelled a free concert they were holding in Stourport because they were off to America on Monday and their gear was packed ready for transit. They will be based in Los Angeles. Bassist Johnny Pasternak said that they hoped to re-arrange their concert as soon as they got back, and thanked everyone who had bought their first two LPs. In the cinema the ABC had a double bill with two classic films *'Butch Cassidy and the Sundance Kid'* with Paul Newman and Robert Redford and *'The Prime of Miss Jean Brodie'* starring Maggie Smith. While at the Haven in Stourport, Mick Jagger appeared in the controversial film *'Performance'*.

Sunday 26th September

'The Strawbs' played another date at Frank Freeman's when they appeared with organist Rick Wakeman. It is their first gig with a new line up before they start a nationwide tour of the country. Kidderminster drummer Robert Elcock is with Wolverhampton group 'The Montanas' who have just released a single on the MAM label called *'No Smoke Without Fire'*.

Friday 1st October

A relatively unknown folk singer, Jasper Carrott, appeared at the Cut Above Folk Club at the Mare and Colt. Described as one of the more interesting characters on the scene.

Friday 8th October

The newly restored Freemasons Arms, also known as The Barrel, was opened today. In 1828 it was home to the carpet weavers union who held their strike meetings there. (At the time of writing, the Freemasons Arms is closed and boarded up.)

Saturday 13th November

Worcester funk rock band 'Pahana' featuring local guitarist Elmer O'Shea appeared at Hartlebury Parish Hall.

Sunday 5th December

Israeli rock group 'Jericho Jones' visited Frank Freeman's. Their first LP released in this country *'Junkies, Monkeys and Donkeys'* was released in June.

Sunday 19th December

Another top group 'Renaissance' appeared at Frank's this Sunday. Originally formed by ex-'Yardbird' Keith Relf and his sister Jane. Keith left recently to join 'Medicine Head'. However 'Renaissance' remain one of the top progressive groups in the country.

Thursday 23rd December

Kidderminster's only large hotel The Black Horse had a serious fire, which caused £4,000 worth of damage. It remained for a short time only as it was demolished shortly after to make way for the new ring road.

Sunday 26th December

Frank held his annual Boxing Day Party on Sunday afternoon with 'Bronco' and friends. This was probably Frank's last rock gig.

1972

1972 was a non-event for live music – nothing really happened!

Friday 4th March

Kiderminster's only remaining cinema, the ABC, formerly known as the Central, was to be split into two with the stalls area converted into a bingo hall. The cinema capacity was taken down from 1,500 to 500.

Friday 7th April

The Gainsborough Hotel opened at a development cost of £130,000. It was Kidderminster's first-class hotel to be built for a long time and aims for 3 star status.

Friday 21st April

The Arley ferry made its last trip when it covered the four-and-a-half miles to Bewdley.

Friday 23rd June

Folk singing stars 'The Settlers' appeared at the Town Hall. They have appeared throughout the UK, the continent, the London Palladium, and have made many television appearances. At the Haven cinema in Stourport there was a three-hour film of the Woodstock rock festival featuring rock superstars like Jimi Hendrix, Santana and Crosby, Stills, Nash and Young.

Friday 11th August

The Shuttle writes that teacher Clifford Ward will have an album released on the Dandelion label, entitled '*Singer-Songwriter*'. A single will be released from it, which will be promoted on Radio One. Also the 'Nonentities' announced they are starting their 35th season at their new home in the recently renovated church hall of St Oswalds in Broadwaters. They opened with a comedy by Jack Pulman called *'The Happy Apple'*.

Friday 15th Sept ember
Folk singer Dave Cartwright from Bewdley also his first LP, entitled *'A Little Bit Of Glory'*. He has been singing full-time at clubs and festivals around the country.

Nothing much happened for the rest of the year. The great wave of rock and pop music that had washed over Kidderminster since the mid 60s receded to the large towns and cities. The groups got too expensive; the equipment got too large. All the venues that had provided such great music for a number of years - Frank Freeman's, The Black Horse, the Park Atwood, the Wharf and the Chateau - all closed down for a variety of reasons. The town sunk into a state of hibernation for a few years until the late 70s when punk and new wave rock exploded onto the scene. But that's a story best saved for another day.

ACKNOWLEDGEMENTS

In this chapter I would particularly like to thank Wynn Freeman, Robert Plant, Andy Silvester and also Rod Gilchrist, David Shuck, Rob Baynham, Paul Jennings, Colin Hill, Robbie Blunt, Kevyn Gammond, Nigel Pheysey, Elmer O'Shea, Rob Newell, Alan Millward, Dave Bradley, Roger Sullivan, Lyn (Silvester) Sullivan, Trevor Jones, Bob Barber, Dave Bodley, David Virr, John Bates, Martyn Price, George Kristic, Terry Edwards.

RECOMMENDED READING

Once again I am indebted to Dave Cartwright's great book about Clifford T Ward - *Bittersweet*

Captain Beefheart - Mike Barnes - ISBN-0-7043-8073-0

RIP

Rob Elcock - drummer (Black Snake Moan, The Simonals, Sounds of Blue, The Rishells, The Montanas)

Johnny Pasternak - bass. (The Javelins, Crawling Kingsnakes, The Shakedown Sound, Bronco)

Abdul Benson - keyboards. (The Reflections, Custard Tree, Wise Virgin, Salamander)

Graham Drew - guitarist. (The Reflections, Cliff Wards Cruisers)
Clifford T Ward - Singer, Songwriter
Frank Freeman -- Dance Teacher, Promoter
Dave Deakin - Vocalist (Big Dave and the Hangmen)

* Every effort has been made to contact the copyright holders of all Tornado's photographs.